The Voyage #3: Panama to the Isle of Man

The Voyage #3: Panama to the Isle of Man

John Passmore

oldmansailing

Samsara Press

First published 2025

Copyright © 2025 by John Passmore

John Passmore has asserted his right under the Copyright, Designs and Patents Act of 1988 to be identified as the Author of this work.

All rights reserved. No part of this publication may be reproduced or transmitted in any form or by any means, electronic or mechanical, including photocopying, recording, or any information storage or retrieval system without prior permission from the Author.

No responsibility for loss caused to any individual or organisation acting on or refraining from action as a result of the material in this publication can be accepted by the Author.

ISBN: 9798268770568

Cover design by John Passmore
Cover photograph: Sunset, North Atlantic Ocean by John Passmore

Author's Note: I believe this book is free of spelling mistakes, typographical errors and grammatical howlers. However, if you spot one – and you are the first to tell me about it – I will gladly refund the cost of your book. Please send the mistake with the five words surrounding it exactly as it appears in the text (so that I can search for it) to john@oldmansailing.com.

This book is for Eric. You'll find out why.

Disasters about to happen do not trouble the minds of those too dim to imagine them.

— OLD MAN SAILING

Foreword

Somewhat absurdly, this book got started before the last one was finished.

I was four days short of arriving in Carriacou at the end of The Voyage #2 - Falmouth to Grenada, and I had just finished reading *Wavewalker* by Suzanne Heywood.

This is the traumatic story of her childhood growing up on her parents' 50ft schooner, deprived of friends and schooling, and forced to act as her mother's kitchen maid. At one point, after hitting her head in a storm, she was made to undergo seven brain operations on a remote island - without anaesthetic.

And all this at the age of seven.

It's the kind of book that leaves an impression - and one of the impressions was of their visit to Tristan da Cunha - the tiny lump of volcanic rock midway between Argentina and South Africa.

I had heard of Tristan da Cunha. I remember the eruption in 1961 when the entire population had to be evacuated (and a lot of the younger people didn't want to go back again, once they'd seen what the rest of the world had to offer).

I was so bound up in the story that I determined then and there (bowling along under twin headsails, the steering held together with string) that I, too, would sail to Tristan da Cunha. I even planned the route - an enormous figure-of-eight encompassing both the North and South Atlantic.

The trouble with an exercise like that is that it becomes a commitment. To change your mind would be, in some way, "chickening out".

Of course, it would mean yet another Atlantic crossing - I

wasn't going to beat into the southeast trades for 2,000 miles. And it would be necessary to arrive in the middle of the southern summer. Then there was the hurricane season in the Caribbean to consider - and among all these natural time constraints, there was the idiocy of Brexit: As a UK citizen, I was now limited to no more than 90 days out of every 180 in the EU.

The problem was that, as usual, anything that appears even remotely difficult immediately acquires a frisson of excitement. Over the ensuing two years, I couldn't leave it alone. The foreword that I began on that passage to Grenada grew and grew. I've just tried to edit it - it was longer than any of the chapters, constantly contradicting itself as I thrashed out the itinerary - and then had to start all over again to incorporate family holidays and my son Owen's wedding...

Quite apart from Central America.

If you think cruising the Caribbean is the sailor's heaven, wait until you get to Panama - and now people tell me it's not a patch on Costa Rica, and "you must visit Honduras and the Bay Islands". Cuba is still unspoiled - but see it now before it changes forever...

I remember one particular day in the Limon Cays of the San Blas Islands: I had spent the morning sitting under Samsara's enormous awning (Raphael in Santa Marta took so long to make it that I had to cancel my Spanish lessons in Cartagena). I had filled a whole page of a notebook with distances and timings, cross-referenced possible departure dates with the family skiing holiday (some things are sacrosanct). I was feeling overwhelmed with all the detail and decided I needed a break.

Now, if you need a break, you're in the right place in the San Blas Islands. They're just sand and palm trees, some of them so small that there might be only one indigenous Guna family eking out a living from the sea as their ancestors have for 500 years -

only now they take their dugout canoes and sell lobster and their intricately-sewn *molas* to the yachties.

Better still, in the Limon Cays, on one particular island called Yerba, there is quite the most excellent restaurant and certainly the best Piña Colada west of Punta Gallinas (the secret is to serve it in its own pineapple skin).

I was on my way there and just crossing the stern of the only other boat in the anchorage when the skipper looked up and noticed my new electric outboard. It's called a Remigo and doesn't look like any outboard anyone has seen before. This means it's a conversation starter.

The skipper turned out to be an American called Lou. His boat was a catamaran the size of a modest Manhattan apartment. He had been persuaded to buy it rather than something more manageable by a woman who said she wanted to sail around the world with him, and then changed her mind about the whole project - as well as Lou.

He looked longingly at my little boat, was amazed that I had come all the way from England. He joined me for lunch.

It turned into one of those five-hour lunches, and I never did get any further with my planning. He thought he might stay where he was. He's probably still there. I did meet a German who had lived on his boat in the San Blas for eight years.

So, it wasn't until I was sitting with the family on a restaurant terrace at the foot of the Matterhorn that the plan came together: I had proposed that we would meet again in July in the Azores after my escape from the hurricane season, but before I could head south for Christmas.

"Oh no," said Tamsin. She was going to Hanoi to visit Lottie (Lottie was teaching English to Vietnamese children). Tamsin wouldn't have enough holiday from her new job to spend a week with me as well. Where else was I going? Well, I did like Ireland…

There were people around the table who had never been to Ireland. Also, unlike the rest of the EU, Dublin has a free-travel agreement with the UK, so I wouldn't be using up my Stupid-Brexit allowance.

At first glance, this allowed time to stop in Cuba and visit my niece in the Bahamas. But then Donald Trump announced that he already had troops in Panama ready to "take back" the Canal.

I could see myself getting trapped by a State of Emergency - and what would happen if ICE took a look at some of my blog posts about the orange one? I would be shipped off to El Salvador before you could say: "Make America Great Again."

I looked up the Price of a Bahamian cruising permit and crossed The Bahamas off the list. An Australian told me about Cuban customs officers so hard up, they confiscate all your food and booze.

That was when I happened to notice a random item that the Isle of Man TT was due to start at the beginning of June. I had never seen the TT. I tried once, but it rained.

If you're not familiar with this extraordinary event, it is billed as "The Most Dangerous Race In The World" - motorcyclists roaring round 37-miles of public roads at speeds up to 180 miles an h*our, through town squares, up and down mountains, 200 corners...

They say that every year, somebody dies - although that's not quite true. But it does draw thousands of motorbike enthusiasts from all over the world.

And me.

I had a BSA Bantam once. I nearly killed myself on Streatham High Road. I wouldn't dream of riding a motorcycle now.

But if I left Panama immediately - and averaged 100 miles a day for 50 days, I could get there for the last race.

And the Isle of Man is only a day's sail from Dublin. Besides, it would give a purpose to the voyage. It would be good copy.

John Passmore

It would be a race of my own.

Day 0 minus one (the false start)

Monday April 14th
Panamarina, Panama

After falling asleep at nine o'clock last night (a combination of jetlag, returning to the no-lunch regime and starting to cook dinner at 6.30, not to mention two cans of Balboa and two glasses of rum), I woke up raring to go.

I would leave this evening - nip round to Linton Bay in time for Fausto to open his immigration office - a quick trip to the fuel station to stock up with beer. Then Charlie's produce container for fresh veg. Collect the new iPad from Felipe. I could be gone by dark…

Now for the arithmetic: The most direct route from Linton to Castletown is 5,166 miles. At my usual 90 miles a day, that works out at 57 days, or 8.2 weeks. Call it two months.

So, depart Apr 14th. Arrive: June 11th.

Too late. The TT fortnight ends on June 7th. So, how many miles a day would I need to make good to get there for the last day: Arrive on the evening of June 6th?

Answer: 99.3.

Call it 100 - 5,166 miles. I could be there on the Friday morning - with two days of the action still to go (in case it rains on one of them).

But what if I didn't go through the Bahamas, but round them to the West? That would save ten miles - more to the point, I would have 200 miles in the Gulf Stream with its two-to-five-knot current in my favour and the prevailing wind on the beam. That's a couple of 150-mile days right there.

Of course, I'm not sure how dangerous it is to sail in the Gulf Stream. The first thing I was going to do when I got the iPad was buy Jimmy Cornell's World Cruising Routes, but now, I'm not so sure - it costs £150 on Kindle and I've just bought a lot of lunches for six people in mountain restaurants. Besides, surely I can find the information online for nothing.

I looked up sailing in the Gulf Stream: Any northerly component in the wind turns one metre waves into two metre waves. Violent thunderstorms with high winds appear out of nowhere. There is heavy traffic with large vessels on autopilot, yachts crossing from Florida to the Bahamas. Inexperienced crews in chartered high-speed fishing boats…

I can decide when I get there.

So, I did indeed get up early and nip round to Linton Bay before Fausto closed his immigration office at eleven. The trouble is, he can't issue my exit permit himself. He has to go to Colón for it. Come back tomorrow.

I spent the extra time in expeditions to the Chinese supermarket in Puerto Lindo. Tamsin and Theo had told me I wasn't eating enough protein - old people need extra protein. I bought peanuts - and more peanuts. I bought 30 onions - enough fresh veg to fill both fridges. I even turned up the beer fridge from 2°C to 10°C and moved some of the cans to the bilges.

Then back to Linton Bay to Charlie in the hope that he would have some English breakfast tea. He'd never heard of it - so it was back to Puerto Lindo for 200 bags of Chinese black tea. Somehow, I don't think it's the same thing.

Then it turned out that the iPad, which had been delivered first to Miami and then by independent courier to Panama City and finally collected by Felipe, was the wrong kind and wouldn't receive a GPS signal. I needed the kind that worked with a mobile phone signal. The helpful associate at Apple told me I could return it.

But I do have a GPS dongle. Maybe that would work. All the same, I saved the box. I could put it on eBay when I get back to England.

Day 0 (The Real One)

> Tuesday 15th April 2025.
> Depart Linton Bay, Panama: 1200.
> Wind: NE 3. Barometer: 1008.
> Distance to Waypoint 1: 382M.
> Distance to Destination: 5,166M.

And so, finally, I set off - stowed the dinghy, dropped the Super Zero on deck to see whether the top of the halyard had chafed (I put a bit of tape round it for good measure) and set off with no more ceremony than you would expect from someone going back to the San Blas now they'd loaded up with beer from the fuel station and low-denomination dollars from the ATM.

What I did not do was make a return trip to the Chinese supermarket for half a dozen rolls of kitchen paper. I'm aware that I haven't made a proper list of stores for this voyage - not like the exhaustive calorie-counting of the Lockdown cruise in *Old Man Sailing*. I suppose I'm becoming blasé. But at the last minute, I realised I had about ten sheets left and the spares I thought were stowed in the focsle turned out to be loo rolls.

Kitchen paper is a big thing aboard *Samsara*. We get through mountains of the stuff, what with engine maintenance, first aid, blowing the skipper's nose…

I did consider delaying my departure, but in the end, decided kitchen paper was a luxury. I had plenty of loo rolls (see above). Also, I had a bag of rags (old tea towels and chopped-up T-shirts). It wasn't as if I was setting off without WD40 or Pringles.

All the same, this is going to be the longest voyage I have undertaken - maybe that was why I wanted to get on with it. I have noticed that the sailors I meet in waterfront bars and beach barbecues all tend to enthuse about the places they visit. I always find the ports seem to blend together. It's the bits in between that I remember - the getting there. The Voyage.

I sent the family WhatsApp group a message: "I'm off!" Tamsin replied: "I thought you were going in May?"

*

Now I know why everyone else is going through the Panama Canal. According to the Windy app, I could expect northerly winds for the first two days - bang on the nose, but after that they would veer. The further north I went, the sooner I would be screaming along on a beam reach in 15kts. After four days, when I turned left for Cuba, the wind would be on the quarter.

But it was the first 24 hours that were going to be the problem: I was driven west - straight into the approaches to the Panama Canal.

South coast sailors - south coast of England sailors - tend to get very blasé about shipping. The Dover Strait, they are fond of reminding anyone who will listen, is the busiest waterway in the world.

I'm not sure the person who first said that had ever been to Panama. The plotter was filled with little green triangles. At dusk, a particularly persistent tanker kept heading straight for me. I waited until he came within two miles, wondering why he wasn't choosing to go one side or the other, then thought about it from his point of view: He was steering a rock-steady course (big ships do). I was steering with the Aries. Each wave knocked the bow down to leeward. My course must have looked like a dog sniffing lamp posts. Maybe the ship was still deciding which way to jump. I tacked off to the east and let him go by.

But if I did that with every ship on a collision course, I would never get anywhere. A couple of hours later, with something called the *Melissa Elena* bearing down on me, I stood my ground.

On and on came the *Melissa* Elena - at an implacable 10.7kts. I was averaging 4.3 - what's that? 15kts of closing speed? It didn't take long. He slipped by a mile to weather.

I decided to go to bed and let everybody else look out for themselves.

Mind you, I did find myself setting the alarm for as little as five minutes. Other times, when the screen was empty, it would be forty-five (and then I would wake to find myself in the middle of Piccadilly Circus.)

Day 1

> Wednesdaay 16th April 2025.
> 10° 68.298'N 80° 0.654'W.
> Wind NE 4-5. Barometer 1010.
> Day's Run 85M.
> Distance to Waypoint: 1: 311M.
> Distance to Destination: 5,081M.

If I hadn't been in such a hurry (the TT and all), I would have waited for a weather window. I now discover there's one due on Saturday evening. Until then, I'm stuck with this northeasterly and being blown in the direction of Nicaragua instead of the Cayman Islands.

There's no immediate problem. I still have 250 miles to go before I hit anything, and I don't really believe I'm averaging the 4.166 (recurring) knots that amounts to 100 miles a day. All the same, I really don't want to go anywhere near Nicaragua. The country is so poor that it's said the fishermen are not averse to a little light piracy to pass the time. A hundred miles off would do nicely.

Day 2

Thursday 17th April 2025.
12° 24.942'N 80° 0.654'W.
Wind: ENE 4-5. Barometer: 1010.
Day's run: 98M.
Distance to Waypoint 1: 226.
Distance to Destination: 4,983.

Actually, we're now heading for Waypoint 2. This is a point some 125 west and a little to the south of Waypoint 1. It's an easier aiming point with the wind as it is, and although it's closer to the Nicaraguan coast, it's still more than 100 miles off. Originally, I had discounted this route because the chart showed a lot of shallow patches. On closer inspection, that just means 20metres - important if you're driving a supertanker, but not much to worry *Samsara* and her one-and-a-half metre draft. Unless there's a lot of wind, of course, in which case the seas could break on the shallows - but I reckon you would need half way to a hurricane to cause breakers in 20 metres. Anyway, I can have a look and just tack out into deep water if I don't like it.

*

Does anyone really empty the last dregs of water out of the kettle every time they make a cup of tea? It took me a long time to realise this, but the inside of my kettle is almost rusted through. I didn't notice until I wanted just a drop of cold water, and it came out brown.

It may have something to do with buying cheap kettles. During the great refit of 2022, I treated myself to "The Mother of all Cookers", a GN Espace. I was fed up with marine cookers made for the leisure market - meaning for weekend use only, six months of the year. I've had two of them pack up just outside their guarantee periods. Then I was introduced to GN cookers - the Rolls-Royce of yacht cuisine (with a price tag to match). These were cookers for life, so I was told.

I realised the fallacy of this statement when I went to pick it up from the factory. They were testing the new electric version.

And sure enough, within a year, I had changed my mind about Lithium batteries bursting into flames, and I now have 600Ah of them and a 2000kW inverter. I can cook with electricity.

Of course, the nice people at GN would be delighted for me to upgrade to their all-electric model, but I just can't bear to think of all that money wasted.

So, I have a little induction hob. I removed the GN's burners, and it sits on top. I can still use the oven and the grill (just the grill for toast, to be honest). If I ever did run out of power, I could put the burners back and do it the old way…

There is only one downside so far: The GN cooker is so huge that when I installed it, I had to reposition the mountings, which didn't leave a great deal of room for stirring the pan without scraping my knuckles on the deckhead. Now, with the induction hob as well, there's even less room - and none at all for the sort of impressive kettle they like to sell you in the better class of chandlery.

I'd been getting mine from camping stores - folding handles, lightweight, and they don't last any time at all. In the end, I started using the small saucepan - and discovered even that goes rusty if you leave any water in it.

The real problem, I now realise, is that trying to pour boiling water from a saucepan into a flask just means that you pour it all over your fingers and drop the flask.

I'm now using a funnel and being very, very careful.

*

Strange how you get used to living at 20°, clambering about the place holding on - and occasionally getting a bit too confident and ending up being thrown across the cabin. I'd forgotten what it was like, but I've had three days of it now. Still, we are making progress (albeit not quite in the right direction).

Never mind, this is actually the shorter route - it's just that it means threading our way through the islands and shallows off the Nicaraguan coast. The islands show up as yellow, the shallows, blue.

…and since this is a contemporaneous account, I should add there was a little interruption there as the boat put herself about. I thought it was just the Aries being adjusted for too much weather helm, but it turned out the chain had come off the clutch.

Hold on, when I went to put it back, the clutch wasn't there. (It's 7.45 in the evening and pitch dark, and I was trying to do everything by feel.)

The clutch does fall off sometimes. It's the official one supplied with the windvane, but designed for generic tillers - which means it's far too big for little *Samsara's* stick. I did have a purpose-built one, presumably made by the wonderful Alfred Maley, who built this boat in 1973 - but I lost it in the Azores.

I say I lost it. Actually, I suspect I threw it away. I can only assume it got knocked off the chart table into the gash bucket and ended up in the marina skip. I cannot tell you what a telling-off I got from the ship's company over that one. We had to sail all the way back with a bit of string holding the chain onto the tiller. It was less than satisfactory.

That was why I was so alarmed when I couldn't see the clutch on the cockpit floor this time. Surely it hadn't jumped over the side...

It was only when I came out again with a torch that I saw it sitting on the cockpit seat. Anyway, now we're underway again - and, I should add, heading straight for a piece of land called Old Providence Island. It's only four miles from one end to the other, but most definitely to be avoided.

At the moment, Old Providence Island is still 35 miles away. So, it won't become an issue until two o'clock in the morning, but at some time, I am going to have to decide which way to jump. I would prefer to leave it to leeward.

It's amazing how blasé one can become about this sort of thing in these days of GPS pinpoint navigation. In the old days of chart and hand-bearing compass, I would never have dreamed of venturing into these waters at all, but the satellites have never let me down, and just now the Garmin plotter shows the island appearing at the top of the screen as if to say: "Yup, the Navionics app has got it right."

Mind you, there is always the nagging thought that Donald Trump could read one of my less respectful opinion posts and decide to turn off my connection. Never mind, Old Providence Island does have a lighthouse.

At least, that was what I was thinking right up until the moment I clicked on it to check its characteristics and noticed there was one of those little white crosses in a green circle that denotes some helpful Navionics user has added a comment.

This comment said: "Not working".

Nor is that uncommon. Presumably, the lighthouse is under the auspices of the Nicaraguan government, which, as everybody knows, is a bit short just at the moment. Maybe the lighthouse on Old Providence Island is not a top priority. It reminds me of the time in 1988 when I arrived off Rhode Island, the first land for 2,800 miles, only to find a randomly flashing light which didn't match anything in the pilot book.

I had a single-sideband radio in those days. I was able to call up the coastguard. A bored voice said, "Hold on, I'll look."

I imagined him opening the door of his coastguard cottage and doing just that. A moment later, he came back: "Yes, it is out of synch."

No apology. No urgency to report it. But then, why should there be? Any vessel worth taking any notice of was equipped with Decca and Loran. Imagine what he would say now - when even people like me have GPS on their phones?

All the same, I am going to have to stay awake to avoid Old Providence Island.

It shouldn't be a problem. I'm reading Submariner Sinclair by John Wingate. I can't believe how dated it is - but then I must have been about 13 when I last read it. Readers who have read my *Faster, Louder, Riskier, Sexier* will be aware that, like every other prep school boy of the 1950s and 60s, my literary tastes were honed on the War Picture Library comics.

Wingate's naval adventures are the same, but without the pictures: All Germans have bullet heads and say "*Donner und Blitzen*". The Brits get into all sorts of scrapes because they seem to treat the whole business as a game of cricket. Never mind, they come out on top in the end.

If that should pall, I have started watching JD Vance's *Hillbilly Elegy,* which I downloaded before I left onto the new (useless for navigation) iPad before I left. I don't think much of JD Vance, but he does seem to have a cracking story to tell.

* * *

The boat is not sinking. I did wonder - and not just because I have twice left the head with the valve switched to "inlet" rather than "close" - which, with the boat at 20°, means that all the water feeds in rather than out and fills the bowl. Then it slops into the bilge.

But even without that, there had to be some reason why, no sooner had I given the cockpit bilge pump its 13 strokes, the water mysteriously reappeared.

I suspect the watermaker. It does have a lot of connections, what with inlets, filters, the pump and so on. Besides, the watermaker is not performing at its best at the moment. It's supposed to produce 25litres an hour, but lately this has dropped to 17. At first, I blamed the low-pressure pump motor, which I managed to run dry for half an hour because I forgot to turn on the inlet. By the time I realised, it was too hot to touch. However, it sounds all right now and, as I have learned: When it comes to pumps, how they sound is everything.

Before I left, I had an email exchange with the manufacturer. They suggested something I hadn't considered: The pump is beginning to wear out. I have a spare, but I would rather not try and change it while beating into a head sea. Even so, how could the machine run for three hours and still not fill the tank? I measured the output once again - yes, 17litres per hour.

It was only then that I remembered the breather. This is a pipe which is supposed to let the air out as the water goes in (and vice-versa). It runs up behind the fitted furniture at the back of the head and is clearly not long enough. It flops about and ends up below the level of the galley spout. Sure enough, the water, which would normally have started pouring into the sink, alerting me that we now had enough and I could switch off, was in fact pouring directly into the bilge.

I was just congratulating myself on this discovery when I went to flush the unit and discovered the pressurised water wasn't working.

If it's not one thing…

*

Once I came within 18 miles of Old Providence Island, it was obvious I had to bear away and leave it to starboard. This would mean giving up my precious easting and distance from the Nicaraguan coast, but I would just be too close to the eastern side and the island, with its associated reefs stretching for almost 20 miles. That would be four hours' sailing, and I would be so close, I wouldn't be able to sleep even for five minutes - well, technically I could. Five minutes is only half a cable at four knots, but the risk of oversleeping at three o'clock in the morning was just too great. Every time I think of risking something like this, I think of Guy de Boer, who piled up on Lanzarote in the Golden Globe race because he went to sleep and left his windvane steering - and the wind changed.

It was the devil's own job getting *Samsara* to bear away. It seems that after three days of being hard on the wind, like a dog that has learned a new trick, she refused to do anything different. Each time I adjusted the steering or slackened off the sails, she came back to 35°. Eventually - it seemed by sheer force of will - I got her to accept a position with the wind almost on the beam, and comforted myself that, if we weren't going in the right direction, then at least we were going fast. With 22kts apparent, reefed main and double-reefed headsail, we charged off at a good six knots, the spray flying.

It turned out to be the best decision. I had two good, one-hour kips and woke ready to close the island with caution and for the long haul up the west side.

It turned out the mystery Navionics user was quite right. The lighthouse wasn't working. But there were a few street lights and there was no doubt we'd arrived when I woke finally at six miles off.

All this navigation, by the way, was on my phone. The brand new (and wrong) iPad is still saying it has moisture in the connector. I really ought to carry one of those aerosols of compressed air. Meanwhile, I'm refusing to unplug the phone in case it does the same when I plug it back in. At least I have a wireless charger for the phone, but how are you supposed to maintain the "sweet spot" when the boat is bucketing about all over the place?

Day 3

Friday 18th April 2025.
13°48.244'N 81°39.540'W.
Wind: NE 4. Barometer: 1019.
Day's Run: 97M.
Total: 280M.
Average: 93M.
Distance to Waypoint 2: 93M.
Distance to Destination: 4,886M.

There never was any sight finer, as dawn came up, than Old Providence Island lying six miles off the port quarter. It always surprises me when islands have hills. On the chart, they all look like sand dunes.

The detour means that I am now definitely heading for the shallows off the Nicaraguan coast. They stick out eastwards and come to a point at the level of the border with Honduras. They're not really shallow by my standards - about 12metres, but they do have some spots with such legends as 7.5m (Rep 1981), and there are some proper reefs as well.

The question is, how well is this area surveyed? The point I will be crossing is only 20 miles wide, and I should arrive tomorrow morning, so I ought to see any breaking water on the very shallow patches - and it would save me another detour. In fact, I reckon that going all the way round it with the wind as it is, would cost me 80 miles - almost a whole day...

This shouldn't have happened. When I looked at it yesterday, everything was going to be fine, we would arrive as the wind veered and just scrape round the end - the wind is due to veer at lunchtime on Saturday, and yesterday was Friday.

Or so I thought. In fact, for the past three days, I have been ahead of myself by 24 hours (I've just had to go back to the beginning of this book, adjusting all the dates). What it means is that I have another 24 hours of this northeasterly. I suppose the thing to do will be to get there and see. At least it will be daylight and I'll be able to see what's in front of me - and I could be across it in four hours. Also, the Navionics charts have proved to be very accurate in the past. It's not as if this is Cuba - a closed society - and probably didn't get surveyed for years.

*

It's taking a little time to get into writing this book - that's normal. The Voyage #1 was an experiment, and I didn't have nearly enough material. I got it right with #2, and that was a big success. I made sure I sat down and wrote something at least three times a day. Write whatever comes into your head. It doesn't matter - you're going to throw away most of it (I'll probably throw away this). Wasn't that Mark Twain's advice? Mark Twain and Ernest Hemingway - follow those guys and you can't go far wrong.

All the same, for the first three days, I didn't sit down and write enough.

*

It's happened again. I got myself all organised. Laid out breakfast on the bridgedeck (oats and sultanas soaked in water and coffee whitener with chopped banana and honey). The fruit-flavoured health drink. The pot of vitamins and supplements. The Kindle. Two cushions. Hat, sunglasses.

I was all ready.

And what happened? An hour and a half later, I was still sitting there, the remains of breakfast hardening in the plastic container instead of being rinsed out. The Kindle unopened. Just sitting in the sun watching the sea and thinking.

The trouble with thinking is that it brings on this terrible guilt: As soon as I think a thought - any thought - I'm supposed to get out the laptop and write it down. The more thoughts I have at the end of the voyage, the better the book that will come out of it.

Worst of all, after the first thought, the next one cancels it out, and then another one comes along until the whole morning is just a mish-mash of jumbled impressions and half-remembered ideas.

It's now half-past ten (I started at half-past eight) and I'm going to have to try and put them down as best I can.

The submarine saga reached its climax last night with victory snatched from the jaws… etc…etc…

I really was most wonderfully dated. All the Italians were "Wops". All the Germans, "Huns". I really must check when it was written. My guess is about 1950 - and I think I have read it before, but it couldn't have been much later than 1960.

I moved on to "Our Souls at Night", the novel that brought us the wonderful Jane Fonda, Robert Redford film of Love at a Certain Age. It turns out to have been written by a man called Kent Haruf, who came up with his masterpiece shortly before he died. It was only after his death that it was made into a film, and the book (with Fonda and Redford on the cover) brought him international acclaim. It's rather a sad story - like Haruf's. But there's a feel-good factor all the same.

So far, the film is very true to the book. I can say that with confidence because I've seen it God knows how many times, and always download it from Netflix just in case I need a bit of comfort viewing.

The interesting thing is that Haruf, like so many American novelists, has experimented. This must have something to do with Hemingway and Mark Twain. All Americans seem to feel the need to break new ground. So Haruf doesn't use quotation marks - neither single nor double, curly or straight. None.

At first, I was shocked and wanted to cast the book aside there and then. I will abandon any book as soon as a character is "sat" at the bar or is "stood" on the bus. Books with people "laying" in bed end up the same way. Don't mess with a grammatical pedant.

That said, I must confess to an innovation of my own. I believe it was Jane Austen (maybe Pride and Prejudice) who embarked on a long two-sided conversation in which she lost track of who was speaking. There was no doubt about it. I went down the page with a pencil marking whose turn it was - until suddenly two consecutive quotations were coming out of the same mouth.

I really should read it again so I can give chapter and verse (but, honestly, some of these writers of classics do go on. Don't talk to me about Dickens…)

Anyway, I decided the English language needed a solution to the problem of written conversations, so I started preceding each character's contribution with either quotation marks or a dash. A nod towards dialogue in theatre script. It works surprisingly well. At least, I think it does.

Then I started thinking about the Gulf Stream. Everything you read about the Gulf Stream is alarming - like a firehose washing all before it up the Florida coast, and heaven forbid there's any north in the wind or it will throw up the most dreadful sea (as if the thunderstorms, container ships and inexperienced sailors making their first dash for the Bimini Islands weren't enough.)

But now I've been thinking about what happens when I first encounter it north of Cuba. It won't be running at its full five knots, but three to four is still something to be reckoned with - and I will almost certainly have the wind bang on the nose at Force 4-5. Maybe 6. This does not bode well.

Then, out of nowhere came the idea of heaving-to. It would be like standing still on one of those moving walkways at the airport.

The more I thought about it, the more I liked the idea: Instead of tacking backwards and forwards, bashing into two-metre seas, I could just bob along with the current. It might even be faster than sailing a stupid zig-zag course. I can't wait to try it: A hundred miles at 3.5kts is 28 hours, then I can turn north and start logging those 150-mile days with the wind on the beam.

But first, there is the note on the chart: "10, Rep (1981)". This is an isolated dark blue blob denoting shallow water (well, reportedly shallow water in 1981), and it's slap bang in the middle of my track. Theoretically, I should be able to sail straight over it. I draw only one and a half metres. I shouldn't even notice it.

But what if it has grown into a sandbank since 1981 - or a reef… I can't help but feel it would be tempting fate to deliberately try and find out.

The boat is steering by the wind, and I keep waiting for a puff to shift the track indicator to one side or another, but it remains steadfastly right through the middle.

And now it's only seven and a half miles away…

Here's some good news: I was able to write all that with the centre hatch open, the wind blowing through the cabin and hardly more than a handful of spray landing on the leeward berth (I am sitting on the windward berth. I'm not that stupid).

Day 4

> Saturday 19th April 2025.
> 16°24.490'N 82° 03.691'W.
> Wind: NE 4-5. Barometer: 1015.
> Day's Run: 99M.
> Total: 379M.
> Average: 94.8M.
> Distance to Destination: 4,797M

Now we're off! Passed the "Rep 10" and cracked off 40°. Suddenly, the speed is up to 5.5kts, and I can have the hatch open without spray flying in!

I wrote that in the early afternoon. Now it's six o'clock in the evening. I've just come below from sitting in the cockpit with a beer and the Kindle. I didn't want to go to work, but I've decided the secret to these books is "writing in the moment" - and this is the moment.

For two and a half hours, while the sun baked down, I sat under the shade of the mini bimini, perched on one of the raised aft hatches - first to leeward and then, as the sun went round, to windward, two cushions for padding against the rail and the backstay.

I finished *Our Souls at Night* (which meant I read it in two days) and started *283 Days*, the story of the Mexican fisherman who survived 283 days adrift in an open boat.

And this was how we threaded our way through the shallows off the Nicaraguan coast - sitting stark naked in the sun with the wind blowing 20kts on the beam and only the occasional spray reaching all the way to the stern.

It didn't much matter if it did. The water soon dried, and every night I have taken to washing myself down with fresh water - I did try just brushing off the salt, but it's not the same.

And so it was that, sitting up there with the evening beer and Johnny Paycheck singing *The Only Hell My Mama Ever Raised* on the little rechargeable speaker, that I realised why I had set out.

For some people the destination is the thing: You can find any number of YouTubers filming all the exotic places they visit, making sure they go on all the local excursions (lost cities, waterfalls, street food) and for the past year or more, ever since arriving in Grenada after the last Atlantic Crossing (The Voyage #2) that's what I have been doing - up down the Windward Islands, Tobago and Trinidad, the ABC Islands, Colombia, Panama...

But after a while, they all began to pall. There was always a compulsion to move on, find the next place. I even left the San Blas Islands in the end (although that took two months). For some, it's not the destination that matters. It's the voyage.

And for some, it's not the weather and the sail changes and the course corrections that matter, it's what I discovered when I went into the locker under the bunk for a new bottle of sauce for dinner - I had a suspicion the choice at the back of the galley was growing a bit thin...

That was when I made the awful discovery that the spout had broken off the new bottle of Sweet Chilli sauce. For a moment, this seemed like the biggest disaster - until I realised that the Sweet Chilli Honey & Mustard bottle was almost empty. I can finish that tonight and then refill it with the ordinary Sweet Chilli. This is called "blending".

*

It is a quarter past ten in the morning. I have been sitting in the cockpit all morning. At nine o'clock I decided I had better go down and write up last night's dream (yes, the first truly splendid outing from reality so far). However, I continued to sit there, just looking at the water going past. At one point, I think I got up to see if there was any reason the tiller was making a peculiar clicking noise, but there didn't seem to be, so I sat down again - and that's how an hour passed, unnoticed.

Enough! I forced myself to get up and go below but got distracted and cooked four hard-boiled eggs. I shall have them for breakfast over the next four days (a fifth one broke, but I managed to save the yolk, and that can go in tonight's dinner). After that it seemed a logical progression to cook five days' worth of rice.

I got to the dream eventually. After all, there wasn't any urgency: I'd had the presence of mind to fumble for the phone as soon as I woke up and make a voice note. Now I am able to transcribe it exactly (and without having to pause to catch up since the recording seems to be full of ums and ahs and befuddled pauses). I suppose this is what I sound like first thing in the morning…

I was back in my old Daily Mail days - the late 70s. It seemed I had just been promoted to a permanent day shift. That was when the real business of the paper got done - and the editor was around to notice you.

And here was my chance to get noticed: A press conference with the United States Secretary of the Environment (they had one in those days). It started at twelve o'clock and it was in Liverpool. How was I supposed to get to Liverpool in two hours?

The Environment correspondent would be going too. He would cover the meat of the conference. I was there for the colour - the "fluff".

To my surprise the Environment Correspondent was John Dickie. When I'm awake, I remember him as the extraordinarily dapper Diplomatic Correspondent - quite the best-dressed man in the office (and that included Nigel Dempster).

Since John had given up smoking, he affected a fresh carnation in his buttonhole every day. He bought it on the way into the office from Buster Edwards, the Great Train Robber, now out on parole and with a flower stall on the embankment.

"How are we supposed to get to Liverpool in two hours?" I asked John.

"God knows." He seemed to be concerned, but only mildly so. Nothing ruffled John - which was all very well for him. He could get the "meat" from the Press Association. But that wasn't going to help me with "colour and fluff".

I went to the station, but instead of the train, there was a motorised hang glider on the rails. We swooped out of the glass canopy of Euston and ten minutes later, landed on the roof of the Liverpool hotel where they were holding the press conference.

The US Environment Secretary turned out to be a rather beautiful woman. She had one of those exceptionally pretty faces that ages so well, short brown hair (very businesslike) and, oh, what a twinkle in those blue eyes when we were introduced.

We definitely had "a moment", as they say. Indeed, in no time at all, we were smiling for the cameras, arms around each other, and was it my imagination or did she fondle my bottom for an instant?

Obviously, I got the full interview with all sorts of personal details which she had never revealed before. One way and another, I had something the editor was going to notice.

What was turning out to be a pretty good dream got even better with the breakfast. Honestly, you've never seen a breakfast like it: Scrambled eggs and smoked salmon. Bucks Fizz, every conceivable type of pastry…

The next thing you know, I am flying back to the office in double-quick time, parachuting onto the roof in Whitefriars Street and sitting down at one of the great big Olympia typewriters we had in those days. My only problem was that I seemed unable to spell the word "ecologist". I could have asked John Dickie, but didn't like to for some reason.

I woke up with an old man's stiffy.

Day 5

Sunday 20th April 2025.
17°18.170'N 82°47.862'W.
Wind: E 4. Barometer: 1015.
Day's Run: 121M.
Average: 107M.
Distance to Destination: 4,667M

It's a good job I'm not navigating with a sextant. I've just had to go back and adjust all the dates again. It turns out I can't have left on April 16th (or even the 15th which is what I thought originally). It seems I left on Thursday the 17th. It's the only explanation: My watch, the calendars on all my devices - even Google agrees that yesterday was Easter Sunday April 20th, and so I have had no alternative but to go back and change all the dates on the first four entries in the log - and consequently the first four chapters of this manuscript as well. It makes you wonder how well I'll fare if they start World War Three and shoot down all the satellites.

Actually, I have no idea whether World War Three is about to start. I have had no news since leaving Panama. It wasn't something deliberate - more a feeling that I ought to limit my data consumption now I'm paying for every gigabyte. I knew that if I so much as glanced at a headline, I would have to download the whole story.

Then I found I was rather more captivated by Mr Wingate's submariners and, after them, Addie and Louis getting through the night in small-town Colorado. Now I feel I honestly couldn't care.

Maybe that's one of the best things about long-distance singlehanded sailing. Today was another perfect day: Brilliant sunshine (so much so that I haven't needed to switch on the wind charger - the solar panels produced enough for everything from the instruments to watermaking and cooking).

Looking back on the day from the vantage point of five o'clock, it seems that I have established something of a routine.

Breakfast in the cockpit (or *au terrasse* as the French singlehanders say) followed by an hour or two with a good book (or a mediocre book, but what does it matter if I got it for nothing on Kindle Unlimited). Then the beer and peanuts - for the old man's protein. Ten minutes of navigation and writing up the log at noon, followed by the highlight of the day: Logging onto the Internet and the family WhatsApp group.

Lottie wanted the Netflix password (She's in Vietnam - my mind still boggles at modern communications). A quick look at the email inbox and then five screenshots of the weather forecast over the next three days, and I'm done.

I don't do lunch anymore, but an hour's sleep and then the afternoon in the shade of the little bimini.

Four o'clock brings me down to write this. Then it's time for the evening beer.

Evenings are different on this trip. The big event is Movie Night - which happens every night. Maybe it has something to do with excitement over the new iPad, but it goes on all evening (with an intermission for dinner). Not one film, but bits of two or even three - I think that must have something to do with my short attention span: At the moment I'm watching Our Souls at Night (checking the adaptation from the book) and The Boy who Harnessed the Wind, which is proving to be quite wonderful. I've no idea why I never watched it before.

It's a bit disappointing to find that, although I purchased the last Harry Potter on Prime Video, it is showing as "download paused".

Having paid one oligarch to buy it, I'm not paying another to download it.

*

I am plagued by bugs.

This is a bit of a disappointment since I've never been troubled by cockroaches, which is what everybody warns you about (don't bring cardboard packaging on board in the tropics).

I did have the rats in Colombia, which kept the blog going for several days until a reader sent me an electronic trap that zapped the poor little blighters with a gazillion volts.

But now the little black bugs I mentioned a few days ago could reasonably be called "an infestation".

They're tiny - no more than a millimetre long, and they're everywhere. To begin with, when I found them crawling on my skin, I would blow them off. I don't really like killing insects. I'm with the Buddhist monks on this - although I don't go as far as wearing a mask so I can be sure not to swallow any flies.

This has nothing to do with it not being very pleasant to swallow a fly, what worries the monks is that, believing in reincarnation - and reincarnation across species - the fly they swallow might turn out to be their Auntie Nellie (who must have lived a very wicked life to have come back as a fly.)

However, it soon became clear that allowing my little friends and relations to get away to bite another day was not going to solve the problem. I started pinching them off - until I realised I was merely annoying them so that they shook themselves down before coming back for a more determined attack.

The only way to stop them permanently was to grind them to death between my fingers - and then inspect the results to ensure there was nothing left but a few grains of black powder. It was rather disgusting. I could feel the carapace crunching.

To begin with, they only attacked when I was sitting on the port berth, which is where I am sitting to write this. However, in the middle of the day, I really needed the hatch open and the prospect of a bucket water landing on the laptop was too big a risk (it's happened before), so I started sitting on the windward berth - and that' where the little black bugs found me.

After that, they found me at the chart table over dinner. The trouble is that I have no idea where they're coming from: They must have a nest somewhere, like the rats - but, as with the rats, it will probably be somewhere inaccessible.

I can only hope that as I sail north and the temperature drops, they'll move on somehow.

The temperature is certainly dropping. Last night, for the first time, I felt chilly wearing no clothes. It was 27°. I haven't experienced less than 30° in more than a year - 35° most days. But then I am 500miles north of my starting point, and it's going to get a lot colder.

For one thing, I'm toying with the idea of a Great Circle route. The plotter will calculate this for me, but only once I have reached my starting point - it can't be used as a planning tool (or if it can, I haven't found out how). For that, I have Navionics on my phone, but that only offers a Mercator projection.

Then I was looking at my progress on the PolarSteps app, which tracks me in real time (well, every five minutes, which still seems amazing). With that, you can zoom out and view the world as if from outer space, spinning it this way and that to suit your viewpoint. The view from space clearly shows that the most direct route from the northern Bahamas to Carnsore Point in the

Irish Sea is up the east coast of the USA and then across from Newfoundland.

And since I discovered the "currents" tab on the Windy App, I note that much of this is in the Gulf Stream. What if I were to ride the Stream all the way from the western tip of Cuba to the Isle of Man?

Well, of course, it doesn't go all the way. It becomes the North Atlantic Drift after a while, and then that gets clobbered by the tides around the British Isles. But the wide blue river meandering through the tranquil backwaters of the North Atlantic is a mesmerising prospect.

Of course, once this idea had presented itself, I became obsessed. I can't wait till midday's internet connection to get a screenshot - and now I think about it, I do have a gnomonic chart of the North Atlantic. Heaven knows when I last looked at it, now that there's so much information available online. But I could draw out a route, calculating the current versus the distance. I might even get several days at the TT. I could try different vantage points - the town square, which they fling themselves round at 50, and the humped-back bridge, where they take off completely…

Day 6

> Monday 21st April 2025.
> 19°21.968'N 83°43.910'W.
> Wind: E 4-5. Barometer: 1015.
> Day's Run: 135M.
> Total: 635M.
> Average: 105.8M.
> Distance to Destination: 4,532M.

How about that for a day's run: 135 miles!

And there seems to be no end to it. Much of the afternoon I've spent reefed with the wind at 17 or 18 knots apparent. Twice, I got soaked sitting under the bimini and had to migrate to the lee of the sprayhood even though it was in the sun. I spent a good two hours up there reciting my way through Michel Thomas's Spanish course.

I have a nagging sense of failure because I still can't hold a conversation - I just can't think quickly enough to do the translations. This culminated in an embarrassing session with the immigration officer at Linton Bay (not Fausto. He was customs, it turned out). The immigration officer spoke not a word of English and clearly expected me to have a rudimentary knowledge of Spanish. I do have a rudimentary knowledge. I've been working my way through apps and courses and audiobooks and even one-to-one online classes for a couple of years, now. But faced with a real person speaking at the speed of light (which they all seem to in Latin America) and I fold up like a wet paper bag.

Truth to tell, I had pretty much given up, and since the Jump Speak app requires an internet connection, since leaving, I've let it slide.

However, while planning my UK ports of call (Falmouth for the OCC west country meet, Southampton for the boat show, meet my sister Georgie in Torquay...) it did occur to me that I could nip up to London for a Honduran Visa.

The Bay Islands is another tropical paradise, like the San Blas islands, but they speak English. Then the British Government decided, for some reason, that Hondurans visiting the UK would require visas. The Honduras government promptly reciprocated and, according to the local OCC port officer, the only two places you can get a Honduran visa are in Guatemala City and London.

Guatemala City is on the far side of Guatemala (which is on the far side of Honduras as you come from the southeast), so if I'm going to be in the UK...

I started looking at the chart. Studying charts and planning voyages has got to be the single best way to while away the hours as the boat sweeps ever north at six knots. Costa Rica is supposed to be lovely too. Shane Acton fetched up there after his circumnavigation in the smallest boat, living on sunshine and coconuts and the occasional dollar from offering trips to tourists.

So, one way or another, I'm going to have to learn to speak Spanish - all I've got to do is keep it going until I get to the Canary Islands in October.

Maybe I could stop in Cartagena for a month of classes at the Babbel school - that was the plan last year until I got stuck in Santa Marta.

The other benefit of a few hours a day of language course is that the books will last longer. I'm rather aware that I'm racing through them and although the Kindle's microchips are well stuffed with a downloaded library, there's not that much new stuff.

At the moment, I'm racing through *283 Days*, the extraordinary Mexican fisherman. For the first 118 days, he had a companion - until the young man gave up, refused food and died.

Salvador Alvarenga continued on his own. He was a larger-than-life character by all accounts, catching fish and birds with his bare hands and keeping an emergency supply of turtles by flipping them on their backs in the bottom of the boat.

Of course, he did have a 25-foot-long fibreglass fishing skiff. Steve Callaghan, who wrote *76 Days Adrift,* was in an inflatable liferaft that leaked. It was thinking about him being head-butted in the behind by sharks that persuaded me to buy an EPIRB in Grenada. Crossing the Atlantic the last time, I started thinking about how few ships I was seeing and wondering about sinking for some reason and having to take to my own overdue-for-a-service liferaft.

Falling over the side and drowning is one thing - that would be my own fault, and it would be quick (well, I presume not much more than a few hours). But 76 days (283 days?) and all because some ship's captain can't hang onto all his containers - let alone falling foul of the zillion-to-one odds of hitting one of the wretched things…

*

People say: "Gosh, alone at sea for 42 days (or a week, or whatever). I can't imagine what that must be like."

Honestly? It goes in a flash. After the first week, the days flip by so fast it's hard to keep track of them. Last night, when I realised it was time to start cooking dinner, I thought: "Haven't I just had dinner?" Yesterday seemed only a moment ago.

But then, is that surprising when I can settle myself in the cockpit with my cushions and my book for an hour - and find that an hour later, the Kindle is still closed in my hand and suddenly it's time for the noon navigation or the evening beer.

Where did the time go?

The time went at exactly the same pace it always goes: Sixty minutes to the hour, sixty seconds to the minute. It's me that's changed. I am now in ocean mode - even though I shall be within five miles of Cuba this evening, and tankers and container ships are gathering around me, ready to enter the Yucatan Channel Separation Scheme.

Come to think of it, that's something of a milestone - the first milestone in this longest voyage so far. I should celebrate. I believe I have a can of peaches somewhere. I wish I'd thought to buy a can of evaporated milk to go with them.

Oh no, I've just realised the Navionics chart has re-christened the Gulf of Mexico "Gulf of America". Navionics is now owned by Garmin, which I imagine is an American company. I expect Trump threatened with the loss of government contracts.

Should I stop using their charts? I have some Open CPN charts, but despite the name, I don't know how to open them. I admit this is absurd and something of a safety issue.

I have one paper chart of the whole North Atlantic Ocean and a sextant with tables for 50 years. But is anyone really going to care one way or another about a gesture by one singlehanded sailor in a 32ft boat in the middle of nowhere?

Which is, of course, exactly how people get away with this sort of thing.

Besides, for all I know, it's all over and everything can go back to normal. I haven't had any news.

Which is the way I like it.

Day 7

Tuesday 22nd April 2025.
221°19.562'N 84°45.641'W.
Wind: E 4. Barometer: 1016.
Day's Run: 130M.
Total: 765M.
Average: 109.3M.
Distance to Destination: 4,402M.

The last two days must surely go down as two of the best ever - in fact, today is even better because the wind has dropped a little. The sea is calmer, making the motion more comfortable and, best of all, today I have both hatches open and no spray coming in - and yet we're still averaging 5.7kts.

To add icing to the cake, when I logged on at midday, presumably the chart updated itself and, in my honour, re-re-christened the gulf "The Gulf of Mexico".

There was a message from Lottie asking how it's going - and I had to tell her everything was a pure delight, and I couldn't think why I didn't do this sort of thing more often. On the strength of that, I went up and sat in the shade with 438 Days, but after half an hour found myself watching the bow wave as it curled away and slid down the side of the boat and then trailed out behind - dead straight for once - now that we're not making any leeway. It really was a perfect moment.

It's at times like this that the singlehanded skipper is given to romantic notions and begins to eulogise about their boat. Indeed, I get so many people commenting on the blog and reviewing the books, saying they wished they could do what I do, that I began to crystallise my advice.

It starts, of course, with the boat: Buy a small boat, built between 1970 and 1990. By "small", I mean between 27 and 35 feet.

These two specifications, all by themselves, immediately lock in all kinds of advantages.

The boat is going to be cheap.

One of the biggest stumbling blocks to people achieving an ambition to go off sailing is money: They think they have to have a pile of money - as much as a million pounds, to some people's way of thinking. In fact, I would suggest you can get going perfectly adequately on £10,000.

For one thing, the reason old boats are cheap is because in the UK - and a good many other countries I imagine - the problem is not being able to afford a boat but being able to afford somewhere to keep it. In the last 40 years, the switch from swinging moorings to marina berths has become almost universal - with the knock-on effect that there is now pressure on moorings, and so the price of those has gone up as well.

As for keeping a boat in a marina - that can cost you an easy £7,000 a year - and if that doesn't faze you, you're probably looking for a boat costing £70,000.

And yet you can buy an old but sound 27footer for £7,000, fit her out over winter weekends and then immediately set off and lie to your anchor that first night. Believe me, if you do that, your sense of freedom will be tangible. In fact, not just tangible. You will be able to taste it, smell it, hear it and feel it.

You don't believe me? Try dropping your anchor in a deserted creek somewhere like the east coast of England or in a Scottish sea lock in the early spring. Insert the washboards against the early-season chill and start frying onions. You have just created your perfect world.

Then consider that not only is your small boat affordable, but everything about her is cheaper, lighter, more manageable - from mooring fees when you do have to pay for a berth, to new sails and the anchor when you've managed to get the chain round the crown and need to bring it on deck one-handed.

I walked the full length of the harbour in Gran Canaria with my mainsail on my shoulder. When my friend with a 43footer needed to get his repaired, two of us struggled for half an hour with the bag between us.

And if you're just starting out on a budget, for heaven's sake keep it simple. You don't need a watermaker - in fact dozens of plastic bottles secreted in lockers all around the boat provides a built-in defence against contaminated water or leaking tanks.

You don't need a fancy plotter mounted in the cockpit. You can navigate on your phone (have an old one as a back-up and a wireless charger for when the salt air gets at the connections).

All of this is going to cut down on your energy consumption - so you won't need to spend a fortune on solar panels and Lithium Batteries either.

And forget full-length battens (have you tried re-inserting them at sea with a stiff breeze blowing after you had to take the sail off and spend the day sewing it back together by hand?)

Do you really need an outboard for the dinghy? I spent three years without one and never found a distance I couldn't row - and that includes two miles across the lagoon at Barbuda into the wind. An hour and forty minutes to get to the other side (only forty minutes back, though).

You do need an AIS. Everyone else out there is going to assume you've got one, so you'd better make sure you have.

Just keep a couple of thousand in the kitty for emergencies and go. You'll be amazed how well you get on - and how many people you meet in the same situation, all of them ready to share advice and practical help.

And, of course, all of us sail on third party insurance only. If your boat only cost £7,000 in the first place, there's not much point in spending thousands more every year on the off-chance that you're going to lose it. Even if you could find a company ready to gamble on a singlehander with no experience, they would limit you to passages no longer than 24 hours at a time. What's the point in that?

The best news is that while all those retired couples forking out £5,000 a year for hull insurance on their £150,000 boats are going to have to spend the hurricane season holed up in Trinidad or Curacao hiding from "named storms", the Third Party Only crowd have the islands to themselves - just as long as they keep the hurricane watch app on their phones and stay within 48 hours' sail of Trinidad.

Oh, I'll have to stop now. My phone tells me it is not 4.30 in the afternoon but 5.30. Suddenly I am on Cuba time, which means I am due on the sundeck with the Spotify playlist, the Kindle and a cold can of Balboa.

In fact, don't I get two cans for crossing into a new time zone? What with the tin of peaches to celebrate leaving the Caribbean and entering the Gulf of Mexico (yes, the Gulf of *Mexico*) it's going to be quite an evening…

*

I am four miles off the western tip of Cuba. I can see the lighthouse on Cabo San Antonio. I have just altered course to the northeast to sail into the Gulf of Mexico and find the Gulf Stream.

It has all been so easy. I just tweaked the starboard rein for the Aries. I didn't even have to adjust the sails. *Samsara* obediently turned her head, noticed the apparent wind had increased from ten to twelve knots and stepped up from five knots to 5.4. The wind charger voiced the faintest moan of appreciation.

Apparently, it's seven o'clock, but according to my reckoning (holding my fingers at arm's length), there are still two hours to sunset - and I've already had two beers.

Interestingly, I've decided not to switch Starlink back onto the unlimited tariff now that I'm close to land. I know I could download the final Harry Potter, a whole lot more books - maybe even try and catch Lottie on a WhatsApp video call before she goes to work in Hanoi.

But then I thought: Everything's been going so well. Just imagine if, for some reason, I wasn't able to get back on "global roaming" - I would have 4,000 miles to go with no weather, no contact. Would it have been worth risking all that for Harry Potter and the Deathly Hallows Part II? I've got lots of books to read again - the whole Nevil Shute canon, for one thing - and Lottie and I always seem to have trouble finding a convenient time for both of us. Besides, there's something rather nice and old-fashioned about messages back and forth with 24 hours between them.

Meanwhile, the Mexican fisherman has just washed up in the Marshall Islands, which is all the way over in the Western Pacific, so I have plenty to keep me going. Dinner is going to have to be delayed if I'm to keep any sense of order.

*

This is turning out to be quite an undertaking. First I had to negotiate the shallows off Nicaragua - the pirates must have been taking a day off because I've just found a note with advice that I should stay 130 miles offshore. In fact, I managed 66. Now I'm looking for the Gulf Stream.

Apparently, just getting round the western end of Cuba is only the half of it. The trade wind blows a steady easterly Force 4 down the Florida Strait, and unless I have some help, it's going to be a long slog (like 300 miles). Of course, a 2-3 knot current against a steady Force 4 (occasionally 5) is likely to kick up a pretty horrible sea but hopefully, it won't be for long before I can turn north and bring the wind on the beam - and that's when I'll really start flying - six knots through the water and five knots of current!

But first, I have to find it. I've placed a marker where I think it should be, but that's still 88 miles away.

I'll know when the water temperature rises. It's been 27.4° for a few days (down from the 29.5° of the Swimming Pool in the San Blas). The idea is to keep heading north while it rises and then, once it falls again, tack to stay in the "sweet spot".

Meanwhile, it's back to hard on the wind with one reef and the hatches closed.

Day 8

Wednesday 23rd April 2025.
22°45.262'N 84°45.063'W.
Wind: SE 4. Barometer: 1017.
Day's Run: 76M.
Average: 105.1M.
Distance to Waypoint: 291M.
Distance to Destination: 4,326M.

That's more than a week we've been on the same tack - starboard tack (which makes dinner at the chart table more comfortable since you can lean up against the engine casing). One day, I'm going to have to turn round, and then all the small items which have rolled downhill into a myriad of secret hiding places will roll out again - or find somewhere even more inaccessible.

Take, for instance, the item of cutlery that disappeared down the back of the cooker while I was washing up: I don't know whether it was a knife, fork or spoon. I'll have to take an inventory because it's certainly not under the cooker anymore.

Anyway, whether hard on the wind, a close reach as we ducked under the corner of Cuba, a stiff breeze with the first reef or just enough to keep us going with the super zero, the "long board" is about to come to an end.

Although I can't be entirely sure where to find the Gulf Stream, best estimates indicate that we should enter the easterly flow at two knots sometime around nine o'clock tomorrow morning.

The forecast is for a moderate easterly, so I'm hoping the "wind against tide" conditions won't kick up too much of a sea.

We shall see.

Exciting…

*

Actually, I sailed right through the Gulf Stream without noticing. I did think the wind must have veered a tad because I was making a slightly better course, but the water temperature rose from 24.7°C to only 25.4°C - hardly what you would call a global phenomenon.

Then this morning it was back down again. Also, I had only managed to get to within 15 miles of the point where I reckoned I should find a fair current.

So, before breakfast - before doing anything - I treated myself to a spoonful of data and switched on Starlink. The "currents" tab on the Windy app was unequivocal: The Gulf Stream was now behind me. In fact, if I carried on going north, I would find myself in an eddy with a counter-current pushing me west.

I tacked (a very snappy, racing tack if I say so myself - until the sheet came off the winch and I had to do it all again the hard way). So, now I'm heading back towards Cuba, and if there's any justice, I should get a lift and then the final tack should take me south of Florida, and I can turn north and go shooting up between Miami and the Biminis at ten knots.

We shall see.

*

Well, I've definitely found it. The water temperature is up to 26.9°C, and my track on this tack is at right angles to the one on the old tack (which is something I always imagined would be normal but never is). Also, of course, I get a bit of extra speed - around 5 ½ knots, which is great when we're this hard on the wind.

It's blowing 17-20kts and I would have imagined there would be a nasty sea - didn't I think of heaving to and drifting with the current? Instead, there's just a really big swell, which is no problem at all - we just climb up one side and slide down the other. It does make life below a bit bouncy, but if you don't like that, you shouldn't have come.

I was so pleased with all this that I even posted on the blog and Facebook - just a picture of the bow wave and a link to the Polarsteps track. While I had Facebook open, I was pleased to discover that I was able to resist clicking on anything else, even though there was the inevitable picture of Trump at the top of the pile. After more than a week of isolation, it seems that I am immune to the news - I did see something in my mailbox about the Pope dying but didn't follow it up. I think humanity would have been spared a lot of grief if nobody had thought up the Catholic Church - or religion as a whole, come to that (Buddhism isn't a religion, by the way. It doesn't recognise a God.)

Out here with the sun and the wind and the only sign that I'm not alone on the planet being seabirds and the occasional dolphin, it's hard to accept the idea of a bunch of deities so insecure that they all demand to be worshipped on pain of hellfire and damnation.

I'd rather sit and marvel at a dolphin.

But back to business: Having found the Gulf Stream, the one thing I must not do is lose it. OK, so I could soon find it again the way I found it last time: Switch on Starlink, open up the Windy App, click on "Currents" and "Find my location" - and Presto! a little blue dot will pop up showing (hopefully) that I am still in the light blue - fastest flowing - sector of the stream.

But I should be able to do it just by watching the water temperature. Once it falls below 26°C. I'll tack. This does mean putting in a whole series of short tacks rather than staying on this one all the way to Havana and then heading straight for the waypoint off Key Largo, but I will get the best of the current that way.

Day 9

Thursday 24th April 2025.
23°38.285'N 84°45.063'W.
Wind: E5. Barometer: 1018.
Day's Run: 83M.
Total: 942M.
Average: 102.6.
Distance to Destination: 4243.

Well, this wasn't on the forecast. I had spent a pleasant afternoon sitting in the sun with two hours of Spanish course, followed by an hour of "Orbit", the Booker Prize winner - another book by the way, which doesn't have quotation marks. Have Americans given up on them altogether?

Anyway, we were making fine progress with 17kts on the nose and the Gulf Stream doing its thing. Not progress in the right direction, exactly, but you can't have everything when it comes to progress.

And then came six o'clock and I was aware of just how much effort it took to clamber up to the focsle and get a beer to swap for a cold one in the fridge, when - quite unannounced - a large wave crashed on the foredeck - and a good portion of it made its way through the unsealed portion of the forehatch and the supposedly waterproof vent (well, no vent is waterproof if it's under water). It was just as well I didn't have any clothes on.

So, before opening the beer, I took a look at the windspeed, and sure enough, there it was up at 24kts. Instead of opening the beer, I put another reef in the headsail - which necessitated going up to the mast and removing the winch handle (I did wonder whether it was a good idea to leave it permanently fitted now the winch is on the front of the mast rather than the back.)

While I was there, I got another wave over me. This time, unfiltered by the forehatch. As I say, there is a lot to be said for not wearing any clothes.

I drank the beer whilst reading about astronauts observing the formation of the mother of all typhoons about to engulf the Philippines - and kept an eye on my own windspeed, which went on stepping above 25kts. That's the cue for the second reef in the main.

I was rather keen on this because, all afternoon, I had been driven mad by the flapping of the mainsail leech. The blocks for the reefing pennants aren't in the right places for the new sail, and I thought I had solved the problem by rigging a snatch block to the end of the boom for the first reef. Now I realise that it needs to be a few inches further forward. I'm OK with the second reef. In fact, I'm sitting here on the leeward berth wondering if things have calmed down - the motion seems a good deal less violent. But then most things seem less violent when viewed from the comfort of the leeward berth.

*

Something else that wasn't on the Windy app is the position of the Gulf Stream. I had placed a pin on the chart at its southern extremity, so that I could be sure to tack before we started losing ground. But the water temperature just kept on climbing: 26.5°C, 26.7°C - 27°C!

Now it seems to be stuck on 27.5°C - although I did see 27.6°C for a moment, although I think that was an aberration. Anyway, I'm staying on the same tack, which has me pointed at the Hemingway Marina just west of Havana. I'll call in there next time (when it's less of an issue if they confiscate all my food).

Meanwhile, I'll just sit here brushing off dried salt and making good progress.

*

At one point in the night, I saw 27kts on the windspeed indicator. Where did that come from? Windy had painted the whole Florida Strait in green, which means "ten to twenty knots". Anyway, I spent the night double-reefed, trucking along at 4-5kts back to the Florida Keys.

The strait is famously 90 miles wide - which was why, for a long time, Americans were so exercised about having a communist state 90 miles off their border.

I wonder what Cubans think now about having a Fascist state 90 miles off theirs. Certainly, I'm going to make very sure I don't stray into US territorial waters - not after what I've been saying about their President. Mind you, I have heard that US patrol vessels are likely to stop and search yachts dozens of miles from the coast - and it's best to comply politely (why wouldn't I?)

In the end, I turned away 17 miles from the nearest US shoal - a full 23 miles south of Mooney Harbor Key. Better that than an ICE detention centre.

So, I spent the evening indoors reading, writing, cooking and discovering that of the 48 films I thought I had downloaded onto the new iPad, 23 are showing "download paused". It's not a disaster, I have them on the laptop and on my phone, but I believe I am suffering from "Christmas Morning Syndrome": I want to play with my new toy *now!*

Also, I see that three of the films which I have partly watched recently, are all telling me they're going to expire in between 32 and 38 hours. Is this the problem I had with Spotify on the way to the Azores? Readers of Old Man Sailing will remember I had most carefully downloaded my entire playlist (something like 40 hours of music) only to find that the app wouldn't play anything until it had checked that my monthly subscription had been paid - which, of course, I couldn't do because I didn't have a connection (which was why I made such a point of downloading them),

On the next long trip, I thought I had got round this by switching to an annual subscription - but all that meant was that the app wanted to check I had paid my annual subscription *but needed to do it on a monthly basis!*

I'm particularly upset not to have Harry Potter and the Deathly Hallows Part II, which I bought specially for the trip (and didn't download on anything else). It's bad enough not having Casablanca and It's a Wonderful Life - both comfort films perfect for cowering on the lee berth while all hell breaks loose outside.

Still, I've got the Glenn Miller Story and The Sound of Music. I'll survive.

There was one thing that forced me out: A peculiar clonking that I couldn't place. It was more than a lazy sheet in the water knocking against the hull - and yet not as loud as the anchor over the side when I've left it dangling in the water to wash off the mud and then forgotten it.

I should add that, when I leave it like that, I'm supposed to take off my hat and place it over the halyard winch. It's very effective in making sure I don't forget the anchor - I feel naked without a hat.

Eventually, of course, I had to go and investigate. The deck was thoroughly wet and I was going to get covered in salt water again, but needs must…

At the last minute, I hove to for the operation. I didn't need solid water over me. Creeping up the weather side deck, I checked off all the usual culprits, lines unhitched from the mast, spinnaker poles on their way to the deep…

Eventually, I reached the stemhead and there was the anchor, out of the bow roller and hanging over the side, gently knocking against the bow. How could that have happened? I had jammed it solidly in a geometric lock with the full force of the 1000W windlass - and then added a lashing for good measure.

The hook on the end of the lashing had come undone, but that didn't explain how the anchor had been able to jump out of the bow roller - I had to roll out even more chain before I could lift it back onto the roller. In future there will be a lashing across the top as well.

Anyway, the windlass is going to have to come off when we get into port - spending a week on starboard tack has produced a great rust stain on the deck to port where the water has been sluicing underneath. Obviously there's something under there that is very rusty indeed. I can't believe it's part of the windlass, an old shackle pin must have got wedged there…

Day 10

> Friday 25th April 2025.
> 24°07.118'N 82°02.812'W.
> Wind: SE 4. Barometer: 1018.
> Day's Run: 89M.
> Total: 1,031M.
> Average: 103M.
> Distance to Destination: 4,154M.

On the great scale of things going wrong, I don't suppose it ranks very highly - not as high as Catastrophic Rigging Failure, or Major Hull Breach.

But now I know why the mainsail leech had been flapping. It hasn't been a problem for the past 24 hours, while I've had the second reef tied down. But today the wind has eased - down to the top end of Force 4, and we'll be fine with just the first reef.

While I was at it, I gave a tug on the first reef pennant - see if I couldn't get it in a bit tighter. No matter how hard I tugged, it didn't seem to make any difference.

In fact, come to think of it, not only was it making no difference to the flapping, it was making no difference to the position of the cringle. This was still as far from the boom as ever.

That was when (these things take time to sink in) I realised that no sooner had I finished pulling on the pennant, than the clutch on the boom promptly let go all the gains I'd made.

I released the clutch. I applied it again.

No difference.

At this point, of course, my thought processes wandered off in a direction of their own (completely the wrong direction, but that wasn't their concern).

The logic went like this:

If the clutch wasn't holding the rope, there must be something wrong with the clutch. Could I swap it over with the one for the second reef (but then the second reef would slip, which would be worse, given the conditions which call for the second reef).

Will there be a chandlery in the Isle of Man where I can buy a new double clutch?

If I have to get a new one sent to the Isle of Man, the post will take forever (remember the part for the Aries being delivered from Amsterdam to Alderney?)

When I get hold of a new clutch, by whatever means, I will have to take the whole fitting off the boom. It's riveted, and my rivet gun didn't work the last time I tried it.

There were other, more complicated (more absurd?) conjectures and possibilities which I won't go into now. Needless to say, the brain cells were soon so scrambled with thinking about the clutch that they never got around to a very neat and simple possibility.

It wasn't the clutch. It was the rope.

Absolutely. That first reef pennant had been doing the same job in the same place since - when was it I fitted the clutch? 2019? 2020? How many times had I tied down the first reef since then? How many times had the clutch gripped that same six inches of rope - with a strain of half a ton as the wind filled the sail? Which was more likely: The clutch had failed or the rope had worn away?

Certainly, before spending £120 on a new clutch, it makes sense to end-for-end the pennant.

Sunday's a day of light winds, apparently.

In the meantime, I've made it off on a cleat, for all the good that does.

*

I haven't been eating enough protein.

Old people need more protein.

This advice from Tamsin, the nurse, and Theo, the doctor. So, I have been eating more protein. Nuts are good for protein - I have four large jars of Planters peanuts - it may even be five. I am only just getting to the end of the first, so that means I should be good for 40 or even 50 days.

Also, I set out with a dozen eggs.

Eggs are fine in harbour, where you can lift them delicately with the spatula from the pan and sit at your cockpit table with toast and coffee. At sea, they spread around the whole frying pan and anyway, you need a knife and fork to eat a fried egg and how can you do that when one hand is holding the plate (or on this voyage, so far, bowl).

Then I thought of hard-boiled eggs, and they are my new favourite thing.

I experimented with boiling four - not being entirely sure of the recipe. "Ten minutes" seemed to figure somewhere, and I know that putting eggs into boiling water cracks the shells, releasing all the white and wrecking the whole project. The answer is to prick a hole in the blunt end with a sail needle kept stuck in the galley curtain for the purpose.

Whatever it was that I did, it turned out to be right the right thing, and now I have a hard-boiled egg for breakfast every day. I did find that grinding salt and pepper into a bowl for dipping wasn't such a great success because the salt grinder is gummed up with damp salt. Instead, I found that Worcestershire sauce works well - or *Salsa Ingelsa* as the Latin Americans have it (not at all the same as Lee & Perrins, but don't tell the Latin Americans, at least they tried…)

I'm thinking that for the next long trip, I should embark dozens of eggs. The question is, should I hard-boil them before I set off? Would they keep longer that way? It would certainly be better than risking all those breakages and the resultant pong as yolks seep into inaccessible places.

*

While I was writing all that, I was thinking: When I've done this, I can go and sit in the cockpit with Michel Thomas's Foundation Spanish Course - *Esso será genial!*

Just as I was thinking it, *Samsara* put her shoulder into a breaking wave and sent it flying in its entirety straight into the cockpit, some of it pouring in through the companionway and filling the galley sink (which was convenient - I had some washing up in there).

At least all this sun and wind has produced lots of electricity: The batteries are showing 100% - the first time I've seen that when I've had stuff switched on. In fact, now I've got the watermaker running, and the flashing light on the regulator shows the panels are still shut down.

All the same, it's not an afternoon for the outdoors. This is tiresome - isn't Florida a holiday destination? But it seems to be taking forever to work my way through the strait against the wind.

This is where the Gulf Stream hugs the Florida Keys and I am having to take 30-mile tacks to stay in it. At the moment, we're heading for Big Pine Key, which is the last decent bit of land before the highway takes a jump of ten miles across shoals and islets to Marathon, which seems to have more marinas than the Solent. This is surprising since Marathon doesn't have much in the way of water. If they call something a "channel", it means it's two-and-a-half metres deep.

*

The mystery of the flapping mainsail is solved!

This is going to be hard to admit, but this is a "full disclosure" book…

When I put the sail back on after the repairs from the knockdown, I reeved the reefing pennants the wrong way round. The first reef went to the second reef block and vice versa. Since this meant that the first reef was tied down far too far forward on the boom, I resolved this by putting a block on the end and using that as the anchor point instead. This meant the first reef was now secured too far back on the boom (hence the cringle riding high and the resultant flapping).

I was working out how to correct all this - move the sliding blocks and their mounts, obviously. But how easy was that going to be after something like forty years since the demise of roller-reefing?

Give the job to a rigger with massive power tools, if you ask me…

And now it's time to reveal the one small addition to this story which I have been putting off: I had the sail repaired at Alisios in Gran Canaria, after the knockdown on the too-late-in-the-season passage from Falmouth. In October 2023.

So, the pennants have been back to front all this time…

Of course I am embarrassed. On a scale of oversights this is like Nelson setting off for Trafalgar and forgetting to pack the cannonballs.

It seemed imperative that I rectify the situation immediately - after all, one more hour of flapping might be the undoing of my precious Vectran mainsail. But I had just spent fifteen minutes taking dozens of pictures of the sunset in case it turned out to be the best one of the voyage and earned its place on the cover (must remember to check and let you know…)

And this was going to be a slightly ticklish job with 20kts blowing across the deck and the Gulf Stream - while not throwing up the monstrous waves I had feared - at least being what might be called "lively". I left it- the morning.

And it did turn out to be ticklish. First, I had to lower a good half of the sail and brace the boom. Then pull the pennants out of the clutches and lie on the coachroof and poking them back in the other way round.

Next, they had to be pulled out of the cringles and blocks and replaced the other way round (without being tangled round each other, the lazyjacks, preventer or mainsheet - I mention all of them because I did indeed get the pennants tangled round all of them.)

But sure enough, I hoisted the sail to a perfect reef (and the clutch didn't slip).

It was a bit premature because I had promised myself that while I was hove-to, I would poke around in the wiring to see if I could find out why the pressurised water isn't working. Normally, I wouldn't bother (who needs pressurised water?)

But, yes, I need it to flush the watermaker.

So even though we were back on course and making good seven knots over the ground round the corner of Florida, I stuck my head under the chart table, inspected, poked, tinkered and interfered with a lot of wires I didn't understand - all without making the slightest difference.

Still, you think I have problems? Every ten minutes, the United States Coastguard informs me by radio that they have received an unconfirmed distress report from an unknown vessel in an unknown location (although they seem to have tracked it down to somewhere 12 nautical miles north of Long Key) and, if I am a mariner in the vicinity, would I keep a sharp lookout.

I don't think I am, and I'm certainly not going to go looking. I'm doing seven knots over the ground in the right direction. In other words, I have found the Gulf Stream and I'm not letting go of it for anyone.

In the end, the best way of establishing I'm in the right place comes from looking at the track and speed. If it's better than I could possibly hope for, then I'm in it.

I did give all the other methods a try:

Water temperature: This fluctuated wildly - 27.5°C when I was clearly out of the stream, 26.6°C when there was no doubt I was in it.

Forecasted position on Windy: Like any forecast, this has been open to interpretation. If I was making progress, I ignored it. If I felt I was being left behind, I treated it as gospel.

"Approximate position of Gulf Stream" legends on the chart: Actually, these turned out to be the best indicator. I just plotted a series of markers and treated them as waypoints to aim for.

While looking for the "approximate position" spots, I kept coming across "East Florida Coast Closed". What did that mean? There were a few "Prohibited" areas and I knew that the seas off the Florida Keys are heavily patrolled because of the drug trade, but the more I kept putting red exclamation marks on the "East Florida Coast Closed" areas, the more it seemed to be impossible to go anywhere at all.

OK, so maybe I should stay well offshore - but how far offshore can you go before you run into the Bahamas?

Quite honestly, I was getting into a bit of a state about this - imagining ICE men, armed to the teeth, swarming over the rail to taser and bundle me off to an El Salvadorian mega-prison.

I got so het up about it all that I actually switched on Starlink in the middle of the afternoon and deleted an uncomplimentary article about the President I had written on the "Opinion" page of my blog during the election campaign.

It was only after that, when I had calmed down a bit, that I thought to look up what exactly "East Florida Coast Closed" areas were.

You're not allowed to fish there.

Feeling rather foolish, I spent ten minutes deleting all the red exclamation marks.

I didn't reinstate Trump, though. It's a bit late anyway. 77 million Americans voted for him, so presumably he's what they wanted. Anyway, there's no way to get rid of him now. I could dust off the piece in time for the next election - it was rather good. But I don't suppose there will be another election now.

Day 11

Saturday 26th April 2025.
24°46 .396'N 80°24.605'W.
Wind: E4. Barometer: 1018.
Day's Run: 97M.
Total: 1,128.
Average: 102.5M.
Distance to Destination: 4,057M.

And there's a milestone. The figures don't reflect it but, after five days since turning the last corner off the westernmost point of Cuba, I am no longer hard on the wind. In fact, you can pretty much call it eleven days of clambering about with the boat at 25°, climbing uphill to wedge myself at the chart table for dinner, falling downhill into the loo, everything disappearing behind the cooker.

Finally, I can aim for the next waypoint "approximate position of Gulf Stream", and crack off the Aries a couple of clicks. The mainsheet traveller doesn't have to sit right in the middle of the companionway any more - and the apparent wind has dropped from 20kts down to 12, so I can have the hatches open. The decks are dry - the cockpit is dry, come to that: I've just spent two hours sitting under the bimini with Michel Thomas and the Spanish future conditional - and I just saw 7.8kts for the speed over the ground.

With any luck, I can keep this going for the next 680 miles to Cape Hatteras. Imagine doing that in four days? I could be in Douglas for the first day of the TT, let alone the last.

The celebratory mood was further enhanced by another milestone: I was obliged to unscrew the floor and dig out two new cases of Balboa (the nation's favourite beer since 1910) - and eleven bottles of iced tea. When you think about it, with two beers and an iced tea a day, it doesn't much matter if the watermaker packs up (but don't tell it I said that).

*

The Internet had warned me that the Florida coast was going to be congested. It was still a shock to be confronted by the waters off Miami. Apparently, it is the busiest cruise terminal in the world: Symphony of the Seas, Wonder of the Seas, Mardi Gras, Carnival Venezia… I had them all milling about me in a blaze of lights. How are you supposed to identify navigation lights on something lit up like a disco?

AIS is the answer (as it is the answer to almost every question). Symphony of the Seas called me up to ask if I could steer to starboard slightly so that he could line up with the pilot boat. I had to tell him I was a sailing boat and hard on the wind. I could tack through 90°, otherwise I couldn't help. He advised that he would make the adjustment.

To add to the confusion were the incessant Coastguard broadcasts - one every five minutes, it seemed - some of them preceded by Pan-Pan. I would love to tell you what it was that was so urgent, but Americans speak so fast - and radio operators doubly so, as if they have to get in a disclaimer at the end of an advert for financial services. I couldn't understand a word, but I don't think any of it applied to me, whatever it was.

I probably wouldn't have been able to hear them anyway because I have the VHF switched to International channels, and the US has its own set of frequencies (like 5/16 spanners and 98.4°F).

Instead, I just sailed on and sandpapered the battery contacts in the kitchen timer because the timer on the phone just isn't loud enough.

Then, thinking this was actually quite important, I switched on Starlink for the third time today and downloaded something called Alarm Clock Extreme.

Day 12

Sunday 27th April 2025.
26°42.848'N 79°42.229'W.
Wind: E2. Barometer: 1020.
Day's Run: 122M.
Total: 1,250.
Average: 104.2M.
Distance to Destination: 3,935M.

Did you see that? "Day's Run: 122M" - and that includes a tack to stay outside US territorial waters. I only count the miles in the right direction. I love the Gulf Stream!

Just now, I'm doing 5kts to the north with the super zero up and all hatches open. The decks are dry, and I just had a double lunchtime beer in the cockpit.

Of course, it wouldn't do to indulge like that every day - I would soon run out. Apart from anything else, I'm just passing West Palm Beach, and it's like Park Lane with sports boats doing 29kts zipping left and right to and from the Bahamas.

Today I was celebrating for another reason. I'm aware that I have been whinging about the watermaker for months. Bit by bit, the output has fallen until now it is a paltry 17 litres per hour (it should be 25). I had a correspondence with the makers in Spain. They wanted me to measure the output: Fill a 20-litre bucket and time how long it takes. I explained that the outlet was 20cm above the waterline. They said the problem was most likely the pump - not the pump motor, but the pump head itself - the bit with the paddle wheel going round and round, pushing the sea water along the low-pressure pipes.

I did have a spare pump head, but it wasn't new. I swapped it for the new one ages ago, when what I should have done was get the motor serviced. Then, of course, the old pump seized up because I hadn't rinsed it and filled it with WD40.

Leonardo and Hermides in Santa Marta fixed it, and with a bit of wiggling, it turned reasonably well. With a calm sea and the sports boats going round me like bikers with an old lady on a pedestrian crossing, I set about swapping over the pump heads.

Basically, this meant turning the cabin into a workshop-cum-corner shop. All the tins from the bilges had to be stacked on the berths. I seemed to need all the tools out - the vice clamped to the companion steps. Allen keys everywhere…

And sure enough, when I got the pump off, I found I couldn't turn it by hand at all. No wonder the motor had been running hot.

Getting the new one fitted wasn't so straightforward. In fact, it took me most of the morning, lying prone on the floor, my head in the bilges with a torch strapped to it, trying to find the holes for the bolts in the rubber housing that holds the whole thing in place.

Incidentally, if you ever find yourself doing this, do make sure you have the housing the right way round. Why do you think they put the inspection window at the top?

The pump ran really quite well. It didn't leak. The motor sounded a lot less stressed. Pressure was up, which was a good sign - but that depends a lot on temperature and salinity and whatnot. The real test was: How much water is it making and how fast?

I have a test outlet for this. Stick the end of the hose into a measuring jug and see how much it makes in a minute. Then multiply that by 60 for an hour and divide by 1,000, and you end up with litres per hour.

Of course, this is not an exact science - especially when trying to read the graduated scale on a plastic jug on a rolling boat, even a gently rolling boat in a Force 3.

The answer was somewhere between 415ml and 420ml. I plumped for 415 - and ended up with a calculation of 24.9l/hr. That's practically as good as new!

I did the calculation for 420ml: 25.2l/hr!

Don't you think I deserved two beers after that?

I woke up to a flat calm.

OK, so the Gulf Stream was still pushing us northwards at 3 ½ knots, but the boat was hardly rocking. The sails hung motionless - and we were pointing in the wrong direction.

I hate this. I think I must have written more about the frustration of ocean calms than anything else. Once, I even contended that No Ocean Calm Lasts More Than 24 Hours.

I soon learned that wasn't true - ask the Ancient Mariner.

So, the hunt was on for a solution. And here is one, a simple one: An electric motor. But installing an electric motor in a 50-year-old boat (52 this year!) is just plain daft.

On the other hand, I do have my little Remigo electric outboard.

The prospect of using this to push *Samsara* when it wasn't pushing the dinghy was a major motivator in choosing it. For one thing, you can charge it from a solar panel while it's running (which isn't the case with all electric outboards).

I bought a spring-loaded outboard bracket, spent a day upside down in the lazarette bolting it on - and then realised I should have taken some measurements: The prop was well clear of the water. So, it was going to have to be a custom-made bracket fitted on the centreline as low down as possible.

But first, I should find out if the Remigo has the power to push a 32ft, five-tonne yacht (more like eight tonnes with everything I cart around with me).

It was clear that today was the day: Five miles off Cape Canaveral was the perfect venue to launch the experiment.

I blew up the dinghy, lashed it alongside and fitted the Remigo, connected it to the 400W folding solar panel...

The whole operation took half an hour. With a bracket permanently mounted on the stern, it would be five minutes.

The Remigo is a very powerful little motor - 1,000W is equivalent to 3.5hp in a petrol outboard. At full power, it will push the 2.3m 3D tender at almost five knots (which can be a little disconcerting). Also, there's the option of a remote control - I could control it from the cockpit.

The first thing it did was to try to launch itself into space (rather appropriate, just off Cape Canaveral). The dinghy canted its nose up 45°, which meant that at least half of the propulsion was being wasted in upward thrust when horizontal thrust is what we needed. Also, being lashed alongside, it wanted to turn the boat to starboard, so the autopilot kept the helm over to counteract - more wasted energy.

Nevertheless, bubbles began to appear in what might charitably be called a wake. There was no doubt we were moving. In fact, once I got the lashings adjusted to hold the bow somewhere near the water, I don't think anybody could have argued that we were doing less than a couple of knots.

I even withdrew the log impeller to check that it was free to spin - but it's clearly kaput. I've got used to judging boat speed by looking at bubbles going past - anyway, what you really need is speed over the ground, which I can get from my phone.

So, I left it running and recorded a video for the oldmansailing YouTube channel (six attempts). Then I sat in the cockpit for half an hour just looking at the bubbles and listening to the gentle hum of sunshine turning into forward motion.

I tried to photograph the bow wave and, when that didn't work, the wake. And finally, before coming below to celebrate with a bottle of iced tea and start writing this, I looked at the battery state - still 100%... after two hours motoring at half-power.

That's amazing. Clearly, if I can rouse myself to shift the solar panel when the sun goes round to the other side of the boat, the battery should still be at 100% at sunset, which is getting later and later, the further north we go - and then a full battery will carry us most of the way through the night. If needs be, I could charge it from the 600Ah of Lithium house batteries.

There is another possibility - the wind might pick up.

But, frankly, I couldn't care less!

Day 13

Monday 28th April 2025
29°00.575 70°38.951'W.
Wind: 0. Barometer: 1022.
Day's Run: 139M.
Total: 1,389M.
Average: 106.3M.
Distance to Destination: 3,796M.

An update on the auxiliary power experiment: After about three-and-a-half hours, the motor stopped.

Just like that.

This had never happened before - and I had been saying how wonderful it was...

Of course, I had never run it for three hours non-stop before. Maybe you shouldn't do that (although, I couldn't for the life of me think why not - and there had been nothing about it in the instructions).

I tried pressing the 'on' button on the remote control - nothing.

I clambered over the side and pressed the button on the motor itself.

It started.

The remote needed charging.

After five hours, it was clear that the little catspaw from the north west was more like a new wind. The ensign was flying - albeit lazily. The mainsail was full. I unrolled the super zero. In pretty short order, it showed the Remigo who was boss. The remote was charged up by now, so I switched it off. Then I climbed down into the dinghy and lifted the prop out of the water.

With the boat doing a good three knots under sail, I set about dismantling the arrangement. I had often thought that if I dropped the outboard into a harbour, it would be worth getting a diver to retrieve it (in less than ten metres, I ought to be able to retrieve it myself). Dropping it out here would be a different kettle of fish - I just checked and it is 1,000m to the bottom. Of course, I had it tied on, but there are times when you have to move the line…

By this time, the battery status was showing 60% (it had been a bit cloudy for a while). However, now the sun was out again, it seemed a shame to put it away without a full charge, so I left the Remigo in the cockpit, still connected to the solar panel propped up against the coach roof. The wind had picked up, and so the Super Zero made way for the headsail - and the dinghy had dried nicely, so that could go away.

It really was amazing how quickly that 1,085kWh battery charged. It seemed like no time before it was back at 90%.

Except by this time, *Samsara* was being hard pressed. We had water on deck - indeed water washing over the bottom of the solar panel and wires all over the place - 12kg of outboard on the cockpit seat…

Or to put it another way, things had got out of hand.

First, and most important, the solar panel had to go away. It's enormous - 1m x 2.4m. If the wind got hold of it, there's no saying where it could end up. Also, it was on the lee side.

Better if the boat was more upright, I decided, and set to roll up the headsail.

It wouldn't come.

I went up to the bow and pulled the line from there - no problem. So why couldn't I pull it from the cockpit?

I had no idea.

Meanwhile, it flapped furiously in what I now noticed, looking at the windspeed indicator, was 17knots across the deck (with the boat hardly moving).

With a good deal of clambering about, untying bits of string, and following wires in odd directions, I got the panel folded over on itself and, if not stowed, then at least in the cabin.

The reason the headsail wouldn't furl was because the line was wrapped round a cleat - but even that wasn't the end of it: The incessant flapping had tied the sheet to the guardrail in a knot so tight I had to get the pliers to undo it. It takes a good bit of wind to do something like that.

When I got back to the cockpit, I could see we had 28kts of wind, and the Remigo was still on the cockpit seat.

So, I got the sails double-reefed and the boat sailing again- rather aware that all the embarrassment had formed the day's entertainment for the crew of a freighter called *Lucky Voyager* (sounds like a Thames river cruiser), which happened to pass a mile astern while all this was going on.

Getting the Remigo back into the cockpit locker while underway was not something I had done before. Part of the difficulty is that, with the Aries steering - or even the Autopilot, come to that - you can't fully open the cockpit lid, so I had to heave-to again and manhandle the thing back into its slot between the liferaft and the NMEA network hub.

And now the wind has veered some more. Three times, now, I have stepped out into the cockpit to crack off another couple of clicks on the Aries, ease the traveller, then the mainsheet, put some belly in the headsail…

I could follow the wind round to starboard and set off across the Atlantic, but this is a race, don't forget - and the shortest route is the Great Circle route. Also, this way, I can stay in the Gulf Stream for another 500 miles - that's if I can find it again. I reckon I've fallen off the eastern side of it today. Still, with seven knots of boat speed, who's complaining?

*

How quickly things can change!

The sun went in. Up ahead were a lot of very low, very black clouds. Then it started raining. Very hard indeed. I cowered under the sprayhood. The noise was deafening.

Next thing you know, the lee rail had gone under and there was a definite howl to the wind. The wind speed indicator showed a sustained 28kts. That's Force 7.

This was about 7.30 in the evening. I had got out the garlic. I was wearing shorts and a T-shirt because now there was a slight chill to the evening breeze. Either I could take them off and get rained on - but I had washed off the salt already, in preparation for a civilized evening (in salt-free clothes). So, I rummaged around in what was once the wardrobe locker and found the oilskins.

I call them oilskins because they are not high-tech Gore-Tex "offshore foul weather clothing". They are the French Guy Cotten PVC waterproofs the fishermen wear (and if they're good enough for French fishermen…)

As soon as I stepped out of the cockpit, I got a bucketful of spray full in the face and noticed two things: It was warm (so maybe I was in the Gulf Stream after all) and also, that it went straight down my neck, so I would have been better off with no clothes after all.

I put in a double-reef, tidied up the cockpit, checked the course and was just sitting under the sprayhood keeping an eye on things, when it appeared that the wind had dropped. I shook out the second reef, let out some headsail.

And then the wind went back up to 28kts again.

We played this game for the best part of an hour, until eventually things settled down to 18-22kts, the rain eased off, it got properly dark - and I found the garlic had fallen off the chart table.

Day 14

> Tuesday 29th April 2025.
> 30°57.818'N 79°13.221'W.
> Wind: SE3. Barometer: 1026.
> Day's Run: 119M.
> Total: 1,508M.
> Average: 107.7M.
> Distance to Destination: 3,677M.

Yes, well, 119 miles for a day's run is all very well - but did you see the wind speed? Force 3 - and it kept on dropping. Pretty much from the moment I wrote up that entry in the log, I've had a flat calm.

Of course, I pulled sails up and down, fiddled with the Aries and the autopilot - they both have their failings.

Aficionados say that the wonder of the Aries is that the harder the wind blows, the harder it works. This is true. It is also true that the more gently the wind blows, the more it becomes like my daughter Lottie as a helmswoman. I used to say she steered a boat like she drove a car: "Oh look, there's a cow. Oo, I like that woman's hat. Did you see that man on the zebra crossing - he looked like a potato…"

I only hope she's better now - she's in Hanoi driving a scooter.

Anyway, without a decent wind, the Aries sees the idea of a destination as a random concept, and the course transcribed onto the track of the plotter as "conceptual art".

The autopilot isn't much better - just more annoying. Without some sort of resistance in the form of weather helm, it has no feedback to adjust its control unit and ends up buzzing back and forth until the control arm gets locked fully in or fully out. Then it stops buzzing and starts beeping. After that, the Aries gets another go.

This continues until the inconvenience of having to stop in mid-chapter to sort things finally trumps the draw of the Kindle.

On this occasion, it was hardly a contest at all. I was reading Orbital - described (on its own cover) as "beautiful", "awe-inspiring", "stunning" and "an extraordinary achievement".

Being something of a philistine where literature is concerned (see my seminal work "Faster, Louder, Riskier, Sexier), I don't normally give the time of day to the Booker Prize, but Tamsin recommended it, and I found it was "an extraordinary achievement" to finish it.

The book follows six astronauts in the International Space Station going round and round the world. That's it. Actually, it's not a story. In a story, something happens. This seems to be one long description of places on earth seen from space, interspersed with extracts from the Ladybird book of What Do Astronauts Do?

Believe me, steering a boat in a calm is much more exciting.

Eventually, at about two o'clock in the morning, I rolled the super zero (you have to roll it just enough or you can't get it out again without manhandling it from the foredeck.) Then I dropped the main in its lazyjacks and went to bed. I didn't feel too bad about that. According to the plotter, we were still going in the right direction at better than two-and-a-half knots - courtesy, once more, of the Gulf Stream.

The last thing I did was to take off the top of the starboard sheet winch and leave it on the chart table.

I would say Lewmar have a design fault to address. Their winches do a fine job of winching - they are, after all, the market leader. But, periodically, the top caps come undone.

This is serious because it is the top cap that keeps the whole thing together. Helicopters have the "Jesus bolt" - a single bolt which holds the rotors on (as in "Oh Jesus" when it fails). The top cap is Lewmar's Jesus Bolt.

The first time it happened to me was coming into Dublin Bay in a sudden squall when it popped off, bounced once on the side deck and then, in slow motion, dived into the sea.

But I didn't say "Oh Jesus".

Mind you, Dublin is a great place to get stuck for five days waiting for a new one.

It happened again just as I was about to set off from Jost Van Dyke in the British Virgin Islands and sail back across the Atlantic in one big hop (which became the first of these "Voyage books").

And then, just as I was rolling up the Super Zero for the last time, I put my hand on the starboard winch to steady myself and felt the top cap move under my palm: "Uh-oh, must see to that before it goes over the side…"

I didn't. I was in bed before I thought of it - but memories of Dublin Bay and Jost Van Dyke got me out to leave it on the chart table.

It really is the silliest, fiddliest thing. I had tried Locktite to hold it - but all that seemed to do was clog up the threads so that now it just went round and round without locking at all.

I was about to pick out the Locktite, wondering whether I had a solvent for that kind of thing, when I thought to try it one more time (always try things one more time).

There you are: One of the collets was partially out of its slot (and to think that I spent most of my life not knowing there was such a thing as a collet - no wonder Tamsin always beat me at

Scrabble.) Anyway, I got it sorted and screwed home like a beauty!

At eight o'clock in the morning, I opened my eyes to see the comforting green light on the wind charger regulator telling me we were making electricity - or, more importantly, that there was the requisite five knots of wind which makes electricity generation possible… and, of course, progress under sail.

I had breakfast in the cockpit with 8.5kts on the windspeed indicator and 6.2 on the plotter (although the Gulf Stream must get the credit for three of those).

*

Of course, the wind didn't last. By mid-morning I was sitting out in the cockpit with a flask of fresh-ground coffee (the first I've made on this trip - heaven knows why), occasionally reading a page from a book called Narrow Dog to Carcasonne by Terry Darlington *in which something actually happens* - a retired couple and their whippet take a narrow boat through the French canals. In between times, I watched the wind come and go.

Mostly go.

An improvement seems to be to brace the boom - all that swinging about adds to the boat's roll, which in turn keeps the Super Zero crashing about, which can't do it any good. Maintaining equilibrium seems to be the secret to keeping the boat ghosting along more or less in the right direction until the next puff of wind comes along.

I could inflate the dinghy and get the Remigo to help out, but it's a lot of palaver, and I don't like the thought of all that rubbing on the topsides taking the paint off. But having it on a bracket on the stern - now that is definitely the way forward (in all senses, I hope…)

*

Hey, I just looked at the time, and it's still not 1130. I had wondered whether it was worth coming down to write that - and told myself: That's what makes these books work. Write everything down the moment you think about it. Don't read it until you've finished, then throw out everything that doesn't "spark joy" - as Marie Kondo, the Japanese tidying guru would say.

Anyway, I did. I wrote 200 words in ten minutes and thought: "My, that's quick." In my old newspaper days, I reckoned on 600 words an hour (which includes one quick read-through). Two hundred words in ten minutes is twice that. More to the point, I'm still on schedule for the morning beer before log time at 1200.

*

It's one thing to have a two-can beer because of some notable achievement (fixing the pressurised water would do nicely), but quite another when you open a second because you spilt the first - that way leads to the unthinkable prospect of *running out*.

Here's how it happened: I was sitting there with only a sip out of the ice-cold can (well, 8°C) when I noticed how much the boat was hobby-horsing - pitching up and down from bow to stern while staying in the same trough. How would that affect the Remigo? Would it bring the propeller out of the water on every wave?

Actually, there was one way to find out: see how it affected the servo paddle for the Aries. I wedged the beer can in a coil of mainsheet on the bridgedeck and went and peered over the pushpit.

I returned to find the bridgedeck flooded with foaming ice-cold (8°C) Balboa.

This was just not fair. It wasn't my fault. It wouldn't have spilt if we had been properly heeled and going somewhere. It was the rolling both ways that did it.

I opened another.

Something else that you don't get if you're going somewhere: A yacht off the starboard side, which is actually off the port side.

I only noticed her because she showed up on the plotter: Morningside (pleasure craft) doing 7.5kts off the starboard beam. I looked. I couldn't see anything. She was only supposed to be a couple of miles away. I scanned through the binoculars, but they're rubbish binoculars. I bought them from the chandlery in Prickly Bay because the overpriced counterfeit ones I bought in the Canaries were even worse.

In fact, Morningside was on the port side because we are now going backwards - that is to say, the boat is pointing at Florida but going to Greenland at 2.3kts. Such are the effects of the Gulf Stream.

I spent most of the afternoon going backwards under a cloudless sky with just the occasional aeroplane flitting across for company. I imagined where they might be coming from and going to (Washington to Cape Town?) Then I sat under the bimini for two hours of Spanish course - after all, I've got all the time in the world, and it does seem that this is the way to learn. I'm now back on the "Foundation" course (after one session of "Language Builder"). Heaven knows how many times I've been through the 165 tracks of "Foundation", but now I do seem to be able to snap out the answer almost without thinking about it…

Filled with good intentions, I found a grommet that was almost the right size to mend the sprayhood frame (I cut it to fit and jammed it in with my fingernail). Then it was the turn of the water pump: All the hose connections checked out (a dozen of them all told). A brand new terminal block didn't make any difference, so it has to be the pump itself.

I read the instructions, which included an exploded diagram (which persuaded me not to try and take it to pieces). I suspect the pressure switch. I could get a new pump in Ireland and send the old one to be repaired, asking them to grease all the metal parts for storage. Then I'll have a spare.

When I bought the boat, she had a spare (the one that's installed now). The ridiculous thing is that, during all the years it worked faultlessly, I didn't actually need pressurised water. Now the watermaker needs it for flushing. This is not an urgent need. The watermaker should survive without flushing until I can get it fixed - but fixed it must be.

Day 15

> Wednesday 30th April, 2025.
> 32°05.893'N 78°13.929'W.
> Wind: W4. Barometer: 1005.
> Day's Run: 70M.
> Total: 4,764M.
> Average: 116.2M.
> Distance to Destination: 441M.
> ETA: 3.8 days = 30th May.

It was H.W.Tilman, the Arctic explorer, yachtsman and climber, who said: "Never set foot on a boat without an onion."

(Actually, I can find no evidence that he ever said any such thing, but I like it so much, I'm going to leave it in.)

Aboard *Samsara*, I have 13 onions left. They sit on top of the little triangular locker between the forward berths (or what used to be the forward berths before the focsle became the shed).

I moved them up there after I found one of them going bad in the locker under the berth. Some people keep them in a net in the shade below the solar arch. I would too, only I have never succeeded in making a suitable net - one that doesn't spill the victuals straight into the sea as soon as the boat heels.

The reason for counting them is that last night, I indulged in the profligate luxury of two quarters of an onion in one meal.

The provisioning plan calls for one onion every four days - but this means that, once cut, they have to be wrapped in clingfilm and stored in the vegetable fridge. A quarter of an onion can get lost in there among the carrots, cabbage and knob of aubergine (when there was still cabbage and a knob of aubergine).

I really ought to keep an onion log: When I embark on a new one, I could note how much of it is left (and whether the half has been halved itself - a count of quarters…)

Inevitably, I end up with two individually-wrapped quarter onions - not, by the look of them, from the same onion, but both rather tired and on the verge of becoming even more smelly as they lie in the soupy condensation at the bottom of the fridge,

I inspected both for signs of freshness. There were none - only signs of decay. By tomorrow, either one of them will have to be thrown over the side. Fish are extraordinary tolerant of rotten vegetables.

So, there was nothing for it: I would have to eat both quarters in one meal.

There is only one dish on Samsara's menu that calls for half an onion: Baked beans with onion and Idahoan Instant Mashed Potato (Buttery Homestyle).

It is my go-to comfort food once anchored securely after a difficult passage. There is nothing more gratifying than to slam shut the hatch, peel off the wet clothes, put up the table and settle down to a civilised plate of baked beans etc…etc…

I remember in particular one such meal after discovering the race off the southern tip of Fair Isle in a westerly gale (well, the forecast was Force 9, but I don't think it was). The one thing I am certain of was that there had been no mention of any race in the Passage Notes in Reeds. As I remember it, I wrote to them, pointing out the omission, adding that it was only fortuitous that I was still in any condition to tell them about it.

So, it was a real treat, after a day of calms, to search in the tins locker for a can of Heinz baked beans in tomato sauce - even Campbell's would do at a pinch. But after 18 months away from a British supermarket, this was a long shot (and don't rusty cans of baked beans give you botulism?)

Instead, I ended up with "Proluxsa", the Panamanian equivalent (with homemade marinade). Best of all, it came in a smaller can than the European equivalent, so I could justify eating the lot, and for the first time on this voyage, the sea was calm enough and I had a following wind, so I could use a proper plate instead of mixing it all together in a bowl - even arrange the mashed potato separately like a fluffy white cloud above the lake of beans - picked out with onion-shaped white horses.

Considering the fuss I made of it, I might have imagined myself as Monsieur Escoffier himself, busy in the kitchens of the Paris Ritz (Zut alors! No Heinz Beanz?)

As for the remaining 13 onions, look at it this way: 13, each cut into 4 quarters = 52 portions. If this really is to be a 50-day passage (and I have completed 14 days already), then in three weeks' time, every day will be a double-onion day!

Day 16

Thursday, May 1st 2025.
32°21.189'N 76°12.940'W.
Wind: SW4. Barometer: 1022.
Day's Run: 126M.
Total: 1,719M.
Average: 107.4M.
Distance to Destination: 3,466M.

A terrible shock: Starlink data is costing me £6 a day. I thought I could manage on about £2 (but then I did finish downloading the last Harry Potter film). I'm not sure how else I can economise.

I don't look at the news or Facebook (and, I must say, I don't miss them.) I do reply to people who enquire about the health supplement - but then I'm going to make £4 if they order it.

Some of these emails end up in the spam folder, so I have to check there as well - today there was one from a man who had been bankrupted because, while he was out of the country, his boat sank and the harbour authorities billed him for £500,000 wreck removal. He wanted to know about the residual income I talk about on the "Money" page of the blog. I sent him what he needs, but *ouch!* Wasn't wreck removal on his third-party insurance?

One gigabyte of data I don't mind paying for is the forecast on the Windy app. I was a bit startled to discover the speed over the ground had dropped to four knots (when I went to bed, it was seven - sometimes eight (Tom Fisher WhatsApped that he once saw 11.5kts in Arctic Smoke, his Elizabethan 33 back in 2017).

The reason for my poor performance became clear at the 1200hrs data download - I had fallen off the starboard side of the Gulf Stream. The obvious solution was to gybe back 20 miles to the middle of it - all very well, but I had the boat nicely settled with the headsail poled out, the preventer on the boom, folding solar panel propped up against the coachroof (the wind charger wasn't helping much on a run). Now it would all have to be dismantled.

Interestingly, on a normal passage, I would have taken the easy option and spent the next 24 hours trying to sail by the lee as I edged, a millimetre at a time, back into the stream. But this is a race - or a Time Trial - or at least I am determined to get to the Isle of Man while there is still a whiff of burned high octane fuel in the air. I gybed (I even gybed the solar panel).

*

I just came in out of the cold.

Now, there's a phrase I haven't used in a while.

I might say: "Must go in out of the sun," or "At least there's a breeze," and "Thank God for the bimini."

But not a word about cold. It's May. We're on the latitude of Casablanca. I'm not sure I've got any clothes for cold weather. Yesterday I wore a T-shirt and shorts for breakfast and then again for the evening beer. What the hell am I doing here, running north at the rate of two degrees of latitude a day?

It could be even more today. There's a Force 5 blowing right up our tail. I saw 9.96kts on the plotter last night - I stood there for ten minutes like a blackbird watching for a worm, but it refused to budge over ten. This morning, I gybed back over to the other side of the stream where the current is supposed to be stronger. It would be nice to record a 150-mile day.

I'm worried about the rudder. In the middle of the night, I changed over from the autopilot to the Aries. I don't like to do it when there are ships about - I imagine the watchkeepers get used to the little sailing boat and her arrow-straight electronic course. Perhaps they will grow complacent and be taken off-guard if it suddenly takes on a random track driven by the vagaries of the wind.

The changeover highlighted the play in the rudder - there always has been a bit of play (it's to do with the fitting that joins the tiller to the rudder stock.)

If you read *The Voyage #2,* you'll be familiar with what happens when the tiller becomes disconnected from the rudder stock (you reach for the string). But this was more fundamental - and hidden from view.

I wondered about the tangs failing, the skeg coming adrift. How do you steer a boat when the rudder doesn't work?

Well, in this case, you have a drogue and attach it with two lines, one on each side, taken to blocks amidships. You can control your course by pulling in or letting out the lines.

Apparently.

- But won't a drogue slow you down?

Yes.

- But if you go more slowly, will the beer hold out?

Don't even think about it.

*

Following the success of my baked beans with onion evening (I have been offered a prime-time cookery show and a three-book, six-figure deal), I would like to present "Gulf Stream Breakfast".

After the eggs ran out, I thought I should add some protein to my morning porridge - old men need more protein. Note that this is not normal porridge. Normal porridge is hot - scalding hot, as Robin Knox-Johnston discovered when he poured it all over his hand in the Southern Ocean.

My porridge is served cold - even refrigerated if there's room between the beer cans and the weeping onions. Essentially, it is porridge oats and coffee whitener shaken up with water and allowed to soak overnight. It can be livened up with things like fresh fruit, sultanas and honey.

The fresh fruit, of course, is long gone. But when I used to make this ashore, I would add cashew nuts. I don't have any cashews - but I do have jars and jars of Planters' salted peanuts (bought in bulk after the protein lecture from Tamsin and Theo).

So, I added a handful of peanuts, reasoning that salt is good in porridge (don't the Scots put salt on it instead of sugar?)

I shook it up. I soaked it. I added a good squirt of Colombian honey.

And what do you get if you mix nuts and honey?

Nougat.

I don't know when I have treated my newly-awakened taste buds to anything quite so wonderful.

And it's healthy. I have that on good authority.

<u>Gulf Stream Breakfast</u>
3 dsps porridge oats.
1 dsp sultanas.
1 dsp coffee whitener.
3 dsps salted peanuts.
60ml water.

Shake ingredients together in a sealed container and refrigerate overnight.

Add a good squirt of honey before serving (in the plastic container to save the washing up).

Day 17

> Friday 2nd May 2025.
> 35°19.949'N 74°22/524'W.
> Wind: SW5. Barometer: 1020.
> Day's Run: 150M.
> Total: 1,869M.
> Average: 109.9M.
> Distance to Destination: 3,296M.

I have been worrying about the watermaker. Actually, the watermaker has been nagging away like a suspect tooth for some months. Way back in Colombia, I pressed the tit and it didn't stay down.

The tit is one of those modern electronic fuses - a circuit-breaker. Forget fuse wire. Forget, even, the little glass tubes with the filament visible inside. With this thing, if the load is too great, it just pops up again. You can try pushing it back down as much as you like, but it will pop back up like one of those moles in a hole at the fairground when you hit them with a mallet. Wait five minutes, and you might get lucky. Or maybe tomorrow…

I wondered if there was something wrong with it, and have been trying to buy a new one in Santa Marta, in Cartagena, in Linton Bay, Panamarina…

But did any of them have a 25A electronic fuse? Somebody had a great black lump of a thing rated at 100amps. I kept looking.

Periodically, it would work. Periodically, it would play up again for no apparent reason. I would try it in the afternoon - or the next day. Out here it's different. Out here, with 3,296 miles still to go, it's not a game. Even at 100 miles a day, that's 33 days, give or take, with no water...

I do have 15litres in bottles in the focsle and 25litres in cans in the lazarette - that's 40 litres (less what's leaked since I filled them).

I have a good deal of beer - say 90 cans and bottles (and the Balboa cans are 355ml instead of the usual 330ml. I like to think of the margin between life and death being measured at 5ml. I bet the directors of *Cevezeria Nacional* never thought of that when they decided a drop more would be good marketing.

The iced tea comes in 500ml bottles, and every time I passed the fuel station at Linton Bay, I collected another dozen, so heaven knows how many of those there must be screwed down under the floor - I just counted another ten scattered about next to the fridge awaiting their turn. We must be up to 40 litres in "refreshments".

Then there's the liquid in the canned food - I always think it's a bit of a con, how much water they add - another couple of litres there…

So, what's that: The top end of 80 litres for 33 days. What was I worrying about?

Well actually, it's not so much the prospect of me expiring I have to worry about as the watermaker itself turning its toes up. Unless it gets its dose of fresh seawater every three days, bugs will start to grown in the membranes, and the only way to fix that is new membranes - at a cost of hundreds of pounds.

Also, it needs fresh water to stop muck accumulating on the pistons - but that can take a year to build up.

Still, something had to be done sometime...

I had given a good deal of thought to what. If a fuse doesn't work, you can just bypass it - but then whatever is causing it to blow might just blow up the rest of the boat instead. I rooted around in the Toolbox #3 in search of an alternative. I did have a spare fuse holder - a little plastic tube with a wire at each end. I even had the fuses to go in it - little glass vials with a wire through the middle. The biggest was 15A, but it had to be worth a try, surely.

I still can't get over how easy it was - the whole job done and dusted in ten minutes (and that includes putting away the tools and clearing up the little bits of plastic from the stripped wires like a good tradesman).

I didn't even hold my breath as I pushed in the second spade connector - I just knew it was going to work.

How did I know? It had to work - and I'd been working on the Karma ever since it packed up yesterday: I got up at two in the morning to reef and gybe to stay in the middle of the stream (no small thing on a dead run with the headsail poled out and the preventer on the boom - all in the dark with 22kts of true wind and a sea to match).

I refuse to consider the possibility of economising with water - washing out the coffee grounds with fresh water, refilling the 5micron filter with fresh instead of salt (it's on the monthly maintenance list and I had the floor up anyway). Sometimes you've just got to go with the flow - trust that everything's going to be OK (a great line from *Forever My Girl.*)

Sure enough, an hour and a half later, the tank was full and overflowing into the sink - which is about right for two days' usage. I switched off by simply removing the fuse - although I had to do it with a tea towel. It was red hot. Still, it hadn't blown, and I don't have to drink beer to survive.

Meanwhile, did you see the Day's Run? 150 miles - and that doesn't account for spending four hours going sideways yesterday to get back into the stream. On the other hand, the "day" yesterday was 25 hours long, not 24.

*

I was about to write up the log at 1200hrs when I noticed the phone screen insisted it was 1100hrs. Sure enough, we had crossed 75°W and lost another hour - the phone noticed it, even if I didn't.

Tomorrow we'll do 150 without any help.

For one thing, it's now blowing a healthy Force 6, and the sea has had plenty of time to get itself organised into a succession of breaking crests (one of which broke into the cockpit when I happened to be sitting out there this afternoon minding my own business and practising my "Foundation Spanish".)

Ideally, I should have stowed the main and set a twin headsail boomed out on the other side - but would it be worth it just for 24hours? Rigging the inner forestay and everything, when tomorrow (at 1423 according to the plotter) I am going to be turning sharp right and following the Gulf Stream as it sets off on its way to becoming the North Atlantic Drift and wafting me effortlessly to Europe.

Instead, I paid out the 90metres of 14mm multiplait from the aft cleats. It really is amazing how this quietens things down: No longer is the boat hunting around through 60°, sails backing, thinking of crash gybes. Instead, we're holding the course, and the motion below would put anyone in mind of running down to Bembridge on a Saturday evening.

Actually, no. What a night that was. We ended up with 27kts of true wind and speeds over the ground consistently over 7.5kts - at one stage I saw 11.2kts! But the warps kept us straight, and by nine in the morning, we had so obviously reached the turning point that I didn't even bother to check. I just shook out the second reefs, handed the warps and set us on a course across the Atlantic.

I think I may have mentioned the idea of sailing the great circle route, but now I think about it, there was a competitor in the 1988 OSTAR who sailed the great circle route - a young man in a small home-built built boat - but of course he was going from Plymouth to Newport, not the other way, so it made perfect sense for him to position himself to the north of the lows where he would find easterlies. I don't want easterlies. I want westerlies. So, I need to get underneath the lows - which means a waypoint 100miles north west of Corvo in the Azores, 1,844 miles away.

*

I'm going to have to get the coffee-making better organised. I used to have an insulated stainless steel cafetiere, but the problem was disposing of the wet grounds. If I shook them into the gash - and then the gash bucket spilled all over the floor (as it tends to do), the mess was indescribable. Since I'm too lazy to replace the worn-out shock cord lashing, this happens regularly.

Then, when I took the Aries to Amsterdam for its first ever service - it was probably forty years old - I met Lean, who operates the Aries Vane Gear company out of a lock-up in the bohemian north of the city - when he's not drinking coffee, that is.

The coffee-break for the Dutch is as much a part of the national culture as lunch is for the French - and every time I turned up, it seemed to be coffee time.

I ended up buying all the proper accoutrements in Leiden market. The trouble with that was that although the splendid stainless steel Bialetti expresso-maker was beautifully shiny on the outside, it rusted terribly on the inside.

Ever since, I've been brewing the coffee in an ordinary flask and then pouring it into a cup (in harbour) - or an insulated mug under way.

This is fine when it's calm, but in anything of a sea, it can turn into a nightmare of funnels and strainers and scalded fingers.

I'm going back to a cafetiere and I shall strain the grounds and tap them into the gash pot.

Yes, I have a gash pot - you didn't know about this. It's a new innovation for this trip.

Since the gash bucket keeps upending itself (see above) and I don't want coffee grounds mixed up with the squashed beer cans and plastic bottle tops all over the floor, I keep an old Ovaltine container in the galley for what we might call "compost" - basically anything biodegradable that can go in the sea when the time is right (like when onion skins aren't going to blow back all over the deck.)

Carrot peelings go in the gash pot - used tea bags and, yes, coffee grounds. Once a day, it gets filled up with seawater from the galley pump and sluiced over the side. This keeps the galley much better organised and a lot cleaner.

Well, it did until last night and the new pot of Nutella.

I'm not very proud of this - but in a "full-disclosure" account, it can't be ignored. If you had to admit to licking Nutella off the engine casing, you too would feel a twinge of embarrassment at having to describe the circumstances.

OK, so I'll accept that I have a weakness for puddings. My family will confirm that in restaurants, I turn to the pudding menu before the main course. I once heard of a London dining club called The Pudding Club, which met once a month in one of the grander hotels. Their dinners consisted of four (or possibly five or six) courses - all of them pudding. I would have given my eye teeth to have been invited to join (although what the Pudding Club would have done with a pile of eye teeth is open to conjecture…)

Normally, on a long trip like this, I lay in a stock of those individual long-life desserts composed entirely of E-numbers. I know they will kill me eventually, but I can't help myself. Some people smoke or experiment with pills in nightclubs. With me, it's brightly-coloured E-Numbers - they're probably no more dangerous than crawling around the deck without a harness.

However, the Chinese supermarket in Puerto Lindo didn't run to individual desserts (although they did offer a very comprehensive range of machine tools and hydraulic fluid in the same aisle as the black tea and *salsa Inglesa*). So, I have been reduced to the nearest equivalent *Samsara* has to offer: Nutella.

Until now, this was reserved for rice pudding - and rice pudding seems to lose its appeal in temperatures over 30°C, so the jar has been open for some years and the contents have acquired the consistency of old-fashioned toffee - you can bend the spoon getting the stuff out (and yes, I do lick it off the spoon while watching When Harry Met Sally for the 847th time).

But finally, the old jar was finished - and repurposed for storing dozens of tiny Maggi stock cubes. It was time for a new jar.

This was at about ten o'clock last night, when the wind had wound itself up to the full 27kts predicted by the Windy app. Life aboard was no longer the sedate passage round to Bembridge. We were now at Alton Towers on The Big One (the day before I had to present myself at the office with a black eye because Tamsin had been sitting in front of me, and when we hit the bottom, her head jerked back, smack into my face.)

So, a spoonful of Nutella was a different proposition now that it had the consistency of hot custard, and I needed at least one hand to hold on as the boat stopped bothering with the troughs and just jumped from one wavetop to the next.

Needless to say, the Nutella escaped. I grabbed the pot with the spoon hand, but now the Nutella that had been on the spoon joined the rest, which was threatening to ooze off the top of the engine casing onto the floor.

This was a classic catering dilemma: Should I leave it (and let it go to waste all over the carpet - to be trodden everywhere else before I got a chance to clear it up?)

Or should I let go with my other hand - and end up sitting in the sink - leaving the Nutella to its own devices anyway?

Maybe I should do the only sensible thing and use my only available appendage to save the glutinous puddle from its headlong pursuit of gravity?

And which appendage was that?

My tongue.

Day 18

Saturday 3rd May 2025.
32°22.472'N 71°27.347'W.
Wind: S4. Barometer: 1019.
Day's Run: 188M.
Total 2,057M.
Average 114.3M.
Distance to New Waypoint: 1,808M.
New distance to destination: 3,225M.

A big day. All kinds of changes. For a start, if today is Saturday, why was yesterday Thursday? What happened to Friday? Have we crossed the International Dateline backwards? This is the sort of thing that might have happened to the astronauts in Orbital (it might have made the book more interesting).

It turns out that the logbook has both last Saturday and last Sunday down as "Sunday". It hardly matters - and I'm damned if I'm going to go back and change everything. There are more important changes to make.

When I woke up at eight o'clock this morning, it was clear that it had been a spectacular night: We were level with the waypoint, which I hadn't been expecting to reach until half past one. So, I just turned right. I didn't consult the chart of the current - who cared if I fell off the Gulf Stream for a few hours? With this kind of progress, the skipper gets a bit of leeway.

And, sure enough, when midday came round, it turned out that over the past 24 hours, this little boat (less than ten metres, don't forget) had sailed 188 miles over the ground - a world record (well, a world record for this little boat).

It seemed impossible. Three times, I checked my figures. But there was no doubt about it. Meanwhile, the speed on the plotter seemed to be stuck somewhere between ten and eleven knots. Nobody would believe this. I recorded a video of the plotter screen to back me up. I recorded a video of the wake - the Aries flipping up and down, correcting the course and taking us at breakneck speed over a sparkling sea.

The new waypoint should take us between the strong winds close to the centre of the lows, and the calms of the Azores High. We shall see - anyway it's all a long way away - 1,808 miles away.

A new waypoint means a new course for the Fastnet and a new Distance to Destination. This is now 3,225 miles, compared to yesterday's 3,869, which - allowing for the last 24 hours' stupendous 188 miles - means I have just shaved 456 miles off the total passage - the equivalent of four days of TT. Who cares if it rains now?

*

I was sitting in the hatch under the sprayhood because it's blowing 17kts across the deck and there's an evening chill in the wind. I had the Kindle in my hand, but I hadn't turned a page in so long that it timed out and reverted to the cover of *Narrow Dog to Carcassonne*. I was thinking of dinner.

Since I gave up lunch, I tend to start thinking of dinner as soon as I throw the empty can of the evening beer into the washing up basket. Surely, it's good to be hungry. The idea that one should never feel hungry must be at the root of the obesity crisis. I'm not talking about starvation hunger - the sort of thing people have to live with in Eritrea and Somalia. No, this is rather more the peckish sensation that starts you thinking of dinner a couple of hours before you reach for the garlic.

Tonight, for instance, there is no cooked rice ready to be thrown into the pot at the end of the process. Tonight is noodle night, which means I have the choice of fish sauce or teriyaki - or, I suppose, soy sauce. I think I will go for Fish sauce. It's wonderfully glutinous for coating the noodles...

It may be that food takes on a greater importance out here as the days merge into each other and there are occasions when you realise you have been sitting and looking at the sea and the sky and not realised that a full hour has passed and you still haven't turned that page.

I did find that the red-hot 15amp fuse has melted itself into the plastic fuse-holder and now I can't get it out at all. I've had to leave the cap off to disconnect it - that's going to be a priority when I get in. I ran another calculation based on the distance to go and 100 miles a day - even though the average is now up to 114, that can't last: We'll be leaving the Gulf Stream soon, and there are calms to come. Still, 100 miles a day gives me three days before the end of the TT, and you never know, I might get four or five if the westerlies do their stuff.

Then I started thinking about breakfast. Last night, while rooting about for a new can of kidney beans, I found an enormous bag of dried fruit. I have vague memories of that last shopping expedition to Charlie's Produce Shipping Container at Linton Bay and throwing it into the basket on a whim. The trouble is, I'm so pleased with the Gulf Stream Breakfast, I can't bear to tinker with it. I wish I had a tube of Nestlé's Milk. Soak it in a Tupperware - it would be worthy of The Pudding Club.

Maybe I should have a change of pudding - and not just because of licking the engine casing: I'm aware that after more than two weeks, I've had only one good dream - and even that wasn't particularly special. Could it have something to do with Nutella at night?

Or the rum - I've been having a very weak rum-and-water, which is unusual on a long passage. I just fancied it - and thought I had a second bottle, but now discover that one's empty. I saved it because Caribbean rum bottles come with those irritating plastic pourers. The only way to get rid of them is to hammer them in with a 10mm tubular spanner - and I don't want a pourer because I need to be able to refill an empty bottle in case the next one won't fit in the stowage hole.

Is it possible that alcohol suppresses the dream reflex? Which should I try doing without first - the rum or the Nutella? Certainly not both at once…

Day 19

>Sunday 4th May 2025.
>37°55.833'N 68°20.138'W.
>Wind: S4. Barometer:1021.
>Day's Run: 150M.
>Total: 2,207M.
>Average: 116.2M.
>Distance to Destination: 3,075M.
>Distance to destination by Great Circle: 2,832M.

Like a monk flagellating himself in order to purify his soul, I dispensed with both rum and Nutella in the hope of encouraging the subconscious. Instead, I nibbled dried fruit while watching The Longest Day.

By the way, surely that is Sophia Loren playing the pretty resistance girl on the bicycle - why doesn't she appear in the credits?

Anyway, I went to bed at about midnight, setting the kitchen timer for 90 minutes and making a mental note to find the heavyweight sleeping bag, or at the very least, mend the zip on the light one.

I woke before the alarm to find we had gybed and were heading for Namibia.

I put us back on course, reset the timer for its maximum 99 minutes - and woke again. This time, we were bound for New Jersey.

And this went on all sodding night. Sometimes the timer would have 77 minutes left to run, sometimes 22. Sometimes I hadn't pressed the "start" button at all.

But I always woke up.

At one point, I was called up to reef - and then to take it out again. The clamp for the Aries fell off. I sat in the companion for half an hour, waiting for something else to happen. It didn't - at least, not until I got back into bed.

Sometimes I got dressed in shorts and T-shirt. Sometimes I went out there with no clothes at all.

If I was wearing clothes, a wave would come and join me. If not, there would be a blast of icy wind.

And then it happened: Unannounced. A total shock. I dreamed a dream.

I was back in Woodbridge, walking through town at night, when I came across one of those lightweight estate agents' boards made of some sort of corrugated plastic - but this one didn't have any writing on it. Also, it wasn't on a pole but had two wooden handles attached to the back.

Not wishing to leave rubbish lying about the streets of "The UK's best place to live - Daily Telegraph", I picked it up. It was awkward to carry, and so I snapped it in half. One half in each hand.

And it was like this that I arrived back home - the old house - the one we had so much trouble selling in The Voyage #2. That house had a 50-yard drive overhung with trees, and very dark if you hadn't left the outside light on.

I was just starting up the drive when I realised someone was following me. I like to think I would have said: "Can I help you?" That would have been polite. But this is a dream, remember, so social mores get a bit bent out of true.

"Out!" I shouted. "Get out!"

The stranger attempted to charm his way round me - took a step forward. I took another step into the personality of Colonel Blimp: "This is private property!"

I may even have added: "I'll have you know." I think I was on the verge of saying: "Do you know who I am?"

We were now at the top of the drive in the parking area (the one it turned out we didn't own after all, which prompted all that legal trouble). I was about to tell Tamsin to call the police when I realised the house was in darkness. She was out. I was alone in my mission to defend an Englishman's castle.

And defend it, I should have to. The stranger now had a tea towel in his hand, and he was swinging it in the sort of menacing fashion of the sadistic prefect at my awful 1950s prep school. One nasty slap from a tea towel and it would be all over.

I looked at the two pieces of estate agent's board in my hands. Surely there was a type of martial art involving estate agents' boards - Tai-Kwan-Do? Ju-Jitsu? Aikido?

I took up my stance. My adversary advanced, tea towel akimbo.

What is it with dreams that just as you get to the most exciting part, somebody puts the boat about and you're heading for Sangmissoq?

And this went on for the rest of the night. At one point, I got out of bed and put my foot straight through the bottom of the boat. Then I was coming into Falmouth, wondering what to have for lunch and almost got run down by the USS Nimitz (crewed entirely by nuns). Eventually, I stopped setting the kitchen timer altogether. There didn't seem to be much point.

I woke up at 11.30 in the morning to find us jogging along nicely at four knots in the right direction.

*

Only half an hour to go before it was time to log on and look at the weather. I rather hoped I was still dreaming: Four days of calms to come, followed by light headwinds - and when I do get to the other side of the system, moderate headwinds all the way to the Irish Sea.

On the other hand, my old idea about the Great Circle route seemed to offer a lot more in the way of following winds - or at least, not headwinds. There was one gale right in the middle, but that should have moved on or blown itself out by the time I got there. Also, there was the little matter of saving 243 miles on the distance to run.

Something else that sneaked into the thought processes even though I kept slamming doors every time it showed its face, was the fact that if I didn't manage to get into the Irish Sea in time to be reasonably sure of seeing at least one lunatic motorcyclist take to the air at 60 mph over Ballaugh hump-backed bridge, then at least I would be coming in from the north west and could put into Galway instead.

Galway is my absolutely favourite place (and that includes Banedup). Also, it is the only port I have ever encountered where the harbourmaster buys you Guinness.

*

Oh, Frabjous Day!

The overheating watermaker fuse finally blew. I was about to replace it with a good stout piece of wire (and to hell with good practice), when I found that the wire just happened to have a spade-type fuse holder on the end of it.

Scrabbling in the electrics toolbox, what did I find (no, not a 25amp fuse to fit it), but one marked "35".

Bingo - and the pressure readings are back to normal. All I have to put up with is a rather large blue spark every time I turn it on!

*

I am wearing a fleece.

What the hell has happened? A week ago, I wasn't wearing anything at all. I found the fleece when I was looking for the big sleeping bag. I found the Musto snug as well - and kept that out. It's clear I'm going to need it. I did put the long johns and thermal vests away again - the prospect was just too depressing.

And yet I look at the thermometer and it says 23°C at seven o'clock in the evening. The sun has been shining out of a cloudless sky all day, and yet I feel cold. I am convinced there is a cold wind blowing. Yet it is a wind from the south. Where in the northern hemisphere do you get a cold wind blowing out of the south? Other than Svalbard?

Clearly, my blood is thin. I have been living the wimpish life of a tropical yachtie for too long. The big sleeping bag says it is designed for a "comfort zone" of 4°C to 17°C. I have a feeling it will do me nicely. I even found my Marks & Sparks pyjamas - when was I last acquainted with those, I wonder?

And there are still 2,817 miles to go. At one point, somewhere in the middle, we shall be at 51°31'N - we haven't even reached 45°N yet.

Meanwhile, it's Sunday evening - party time on the beach back in the San Blas. At 250 miles off the coast of Massachusetts, I closed the hatch and hoped for a fug.

Day 20

Monday 5th May 2025.
39°07.916'N 66°06.342'W.
Wind: SE3. Barometer: 1025.
Day's Run: 128M.
Total: 2,385M.
Average: 116.7M.
Distance to Destination: 2,714M.

Four good things that happened today:

I found another bottle of rum that I didn't know I had.

The Spanish phrase for "to chuckle" translates as "to laugh inside your teeth" - isn't that wonderful?

I fixed the sticking key on the clarinet. I don't know what it's called, but it's one of the oblong ones on the side for the little finger of the left hand - the upper one. I hadn't taken the clarinet out of its case since we left Panama. Clearly, this was a mistake.

Normally the instrument lives in a custom-made bracket on the mast support, ready for instant action. But I had put it away because it can get knocked about at sea - and then thought that if I didn't keep practising, I'd forget everything.

So, when I did get it out, not only was it looking very sad and I had to polish up all the silver plate, but then it needed a liberal application of cork grease before I could put it together - and finally, it wouldn't play - nothing but squeaks and honks. I kept on trying while the Bluetooth speaker played through a whole rendition of Woody Allen and Pappy's Bb Blues (6mins 54secs).

Then, when I realised the key wasn't moving, it took another session with sewing machine oil to get it going.

I'm not sure if that qualifies as good news. The next item certainly doesn't.

Remember those little black bugs - the tiny ones that I would pinch off my skin and grind between my fingers to make sure they wouldn't bother me again?

It's not so easy when they crawl across the screen of the Kindle. The *Narrow Dog to Carcassonne* had just reached Armentières when I saw my chance and stabbed at the little blighter with a forefinger.

I missed - and the book jumped forward two pages.

But enough of looking on the bright side. The infestation is now a serious problem. It has spread to the galley. After one evening of noodles - and last night's spaghetti triumph: red pesto, peas in coconut milk and dill pickles (I don't know what else to do with them now that I don't have lunch) - and the peas were a bit of a surprise. The label just said *guisantes,* and Google Translate doesn't work out here.

Anyway, it was time to boil up a big saucepan of rice to last for the next five days. It keeps very well in the fridge and - this being brown rice, which takes 20 minutes to cook - you don't want to be doing that every night.

I opened the bag, counted ten dessert spoonfuls into the bowl - and then looked at it. You have probably seen on the supermarket shelf that you can buy brown rice with occasional grains of black rice - this gives the dish a pleasing, speckled appearance.

These were not that kind of black specks.

These were moving.

And they weren't occasional.

Not to put too fine a point on it, my dinner was crawling with bugs - hundreds of them. I began trying to pick them out, but they've been practising their avoidance tactics on my knees, and they were just too quick for me.

All right then, I scowled at the bowl. "If you want to play it that way, I'll drown you!

I tipped the bowl into a saucepan and filled it with water. Aha! They could swim - but that just meant I could just scoop them up with a spoon.

Not so easy, actually - and it turned out that most of them couldn't swim. They just sank to the bottom with the rice. Also, the water was pretty murky with chewed-up rice and other "matter" that I didn't care to think about. I changed the water. Three times. What was left, I boiled it for 20 minutes - bug risotto.

Actually, cooking improved things a lot. Quite a few of the more intelligent little chaps had realised the game was up and made a bid for freedom - only to find themselves welded to the lid and therefore removed from the recipe. Their chums still gave the rice that speckled look, but at least there were fewer specks, and they weren't moving. I tried a small helping - it tasted perfectly all right. With added protein too!

This does mean I will have to swallow my vegetarian principles (if you get my drift), but what choice do I have - and there's plenty of chilli sauce…

Meanwhile, I still have another two kilos of rice and, peering through the plastic packets, it is clear that these are infested too - and by the time I get to open them, they will be positively overrun. A half kilo of cous-cous is the same.

I had thought of deep-sixing the lot, but it's not so easy to pop to the shops out here and, by Day 50, I might be very grateful - bugs or no bugs. Nelson never complained about weevils in the ship's biscuits. So, I quarantined those bags in the tins locker (the little blighters aren't going to nibble their way into a can of kidney beans).

Meanwhile, it was time to look at alternatives. Apparently, little black bugs do not have a taste for noodles, spaghetti or instant mashed potato (or, if they do, then the Idahoan mashed potato company is well aware of it and constructed their bullet-proof packaging accordingly).

I have six meals worth of noodles, eight of spaghetti and seven of mashed potato - 21 days in all.

As of today, if I keep to the schedule, all I have to do is survive for 30 days before arriving at the nearest Indian restaurant to the harbour in Douglas.

Also, I do have 1.7kg of porridge oats - but that's for breakfast, although I suppose it could thicken a stew at a pinch.

The problem, I now realise, is my compulsion to be prepared for all eventualities. I keep the boat fully stocked at all times - heaven knows why. I suppose I imagine myself putting to sea at a moment's notice like Hornblower when the French fleet appears on the horizon.

Well, in future I am just going to be well stocked with tins and beer and bullet-proof mashed potato.

But only enough rice to see me through to the next supermarket.

*

It's an odd moment when you're in a situation which a lot of people would consider intolerable, and yet suddenly you stop what you're doing and think: "My word, I'm happy."

I just did that.

I had woken at 5.30 in the morning to find the boat labouring under full sail. We were hard on the wind about 200 miles southwest of Nova Scotia, and it was blowing 20kts across the deck. This wouldn't do at all, so I changed out of pyjamas, which I want to keep dry, into shorts and a T-shirt. Although they were salty, they were at least dry. Two reefs in the headsail seemed to quieten things down a bit. I did consider a reef for the main, but decided to wait and see how we got on.

Half an hour later, I was up again to reef the main after all - actually, I quite enjoy what always used to be a chore: When you've got something really well organised, it does become a pleasure.

Here's how it works now:

First stop the boat. You're much less likely to get wet if you're not going anywhere - and since reefing is a two-handed operation, if you are going to fall over because you're not holding on, then at least the boat isn't going to sail off without you.

The stopping process is a sort of heaving-to: First, release the main and flake the whole sheet onto the cockpit floor so it can run as much as it likes. By this time, the boat has slowed down considerably.

Next, disconnect the helm from the self-steering and ease it down so the boat begins to come up into the wind and loses way. This has to be done carefully - you don't want to tack. Once the speed has dropped right away, lash the helm a-lee. Now she will sit there, mainsail flapping and pushing the bow up, headsail filled and holding it down. She will sit like that indefinitely, slowly fore-reaching.

Next, ease the main halyard until the first mark is just off the winch. This length of white whipping twine is sewn into the halyard at exactly the spot to allow the luff cringle on the first reef to be lashed down to the gooseneck. I used to have reefing horns like everyone else until the gooseneck broke in the knockdown described in The Voyage #2. In the old days, by the time I got back to the cockpit to take up the halyard, the ring would have fallen off the horn. Now I have a much better system - a line clipped onto a ring on the leeward side of the mast passes through the two reefing rings and down to a cleat on the windward side. That's not going to fall off anything.

And now for the big difference: In the old days, I would go back to the cockpit and winch up the halyard - and then return to the mast to winch in the leech pennant.

Now, I stay at the mast and pull on both pennants - first and second reefs equally. Because the halyard is still loose and the sail is flapping free, this can be done without winching. Coil and hook the extra length of the pennants to the cleat and return to the cockpit.

Finally, make up the halyard, reset the self-steering and haul in the mainsheet.

All done in five minutes with one trip to the mast - and quite often, without getting wet.

Well, I say that. Once the boat starts moving again, there's bound to be a bit of spray. I avoid it by sitting on the leeward cockpit seat, well under the sprayhood, to pull on the mainsheet. However, this morning, the seat was wet, and so I did it standing up with one foot on the seat - and got soaked all down my back.

Never mind, I am now sitting on the leeward berth in a dry T-shirt, listening to old Beatles tracks and have declared that life is too short to read boring books. I was 42% of the way through the Narrow Dog to Carcassonne and realised it was just more and more of the same. Of course, people might come to an identical conclusion about my book - but I don't care. I'm enjoying myself.

And look: The wind has veered. A click on the port rein of the Aries and she'll be that much freer. Maybe she won't hammer so hard. It would be nice to make tea without spilling half of it.

Day 21

Tuesday 6th May 2025.
40°09.332'N 64°03.009'W.
Wind: SE4. Barometer: 1030.
Day's Run: 124M.
Total: 2,459 M.
Average: 117.1M.
Distance to Destination: 2,590M.

I'm not sure this "no lunch" regime is working so well. It might be all right for The King, but I expect he gets more sleep than I do. Yesterday, I wrote about how good it was to be hungry when you sat down to dinner.

Not so good when you're hungry at two o'clock. I helped myself to a couple of peanuts - mindful that if peanuts become snacks, there won't be any for the splendid Gulf Stream Breakfast.

Then I dipped into the dried fruit packet for an apricot.

After that, all self-control went out the window, and I guzzled a spoonful of Nutella.

None of this helped.

There was nothing else for it. I would have to have lunch (it was now three o'clock and I was wasting away). I excavated the packets locker and found a Cup-a-Soup.

Cup-a-soup is a British weakness - a packet of dried E-numbers and an appetising picture. What I had here was not quite the same: Manufactured by Nestlé in the Dominican Republic and distributed through their subsidiary in Trinidad and Tobago.

In the UK, everyone knows how to make Cup-a-Soup. It's part of the National Curriculum. You empty the contents into your favourite mug, add boiling water, stir and wait four minutes for it to reconstitute itself into

heartwarming and flavoursome sustenance.

Maggi Dehydrated Vegetable Flavour Soup Mix, which is what I had here, isn't like that. The cooking instructions show a casserole dish and suggest 7-10 minutes. Also, they don't say how much water.

But I didn't read them anyway. I did it the way I've always done it.

It had the consistency of suet pudding and so much salt it made your eyes water.

I had to have another spoonful of Nutella to recover.

Something else: How long ago was it that I was complaining about having to wear clothes? Now I'm swaddled in three layers, including long trousers, socks and a woolly hat - and I'm thinking I should have added long johns. It's 17°C in the cabin, but there's a bitter wind outside and the sea is down to 10°. It's a different world. This morning I had fog!

Well, I would do, wouldn't I? The Grand Banks are just up ahead. I hadn't really thought much about the Grand Banks. I was last there in 1988 and nearly got run down by a trawler. But that won't happen this time. This time we'll both have AIS. I'll see him at 15 miles, and he'll think life will be a lot easier if he stays out of my way. At least, I hope that's what he'll think.

I'm not sure about the icebergs, though. The Titanic was on its way from the Fastnet Rock to a waypoint about 200 miles southwest of Nova Scotia…

I got out the passage chart for the North Atlantic. It had a red dotted line extending 300 miles south of the Grand Banks.

And a note alongside it.

The note said: "Obtain latest ice reports."

I don't care how many gigabytes it's going to cost. I'd look pretty silly if I went the way of the Titanic just because I begrudged Elon Musk taking my Starlink subscription and sending it to Nigel Farage.

It's all right. The North American Iceberg Service daily bulletin says the southernmost limit is 48°N. I won't be going that far up. I could hit a growler, of course. A growler could be bigger than *Samsara* and ten times as heavy, being 90% underwater. I'm not sure what I'm supposed to do about that. Other than not think about it.

There was something else on the chart of the Grand Banks: "Platforms". I hadn't considered "Platforms". Given that the water is only 30 metres deep in places, it stands to reason that somebody would go there looking for gas, but Navionics doesn't show any detail because my subscription doesn't cover the US and Canada. That would be another £39.99.

I can't believe I begrudged paying it. In the days when we bought paper charts, they were £27 each. Yet, with one tap, I can access hundreds of charts (thousands of them). I paid up - and sure enough, the Hibernia field showed up with two platforms bang on my track.

Just as interesting, it did not show a series of deep-sea buoys marked on the paper chart. I looked them up on the National Data Buoy Centre (which Elon doesn't seem to have got around to closing down - or if he has, his 24-year-old computer geek minions forgot to wipe the website.) The buoys were all there - the East Scotia Slope, the Banquereau Banks, the Tail of the Bank - all with their positions and automatic weather reports. I plotted them with exclamation marks. My track goes straight through the lot - as well as the Hibernia platforms.

Day 22

> Wednesday 7th May 2025.
> 41°19.918'N 61°48.052'W.
> Wind: S4. Barometer: 1025.
> Day's Run: 138M.
> Total: 2,697M.
> Average: 122.6M.
> Distance to Destination: 2,352M.

Suddenly, it doesn't seem so hard at all. Last night, after the first 90 minutes, I didn't set any more alarms.

I don't know when I last had a ship within sight - even the AIS has only picked up a couple at about 15 miles. All the fishing boats seem to be inshore, and I don't know what another yacht would be doing out here. So, I peeled off all the layers, put on pyjamas and zipped myself like a mummy into the heavy-duty sleeping bag. It was 13°C in the cabin.

I woke two or three times out of habit, but the wind stayed steady on a close reach at about 15kts, and we stuck to the course like glue.

In the morning, I made up for yesterday's deficiency with long johns as well as the three layers on top (proper thermal vest this time) and spent the morning sitting out in bright sunshine, not caring about the icy wind and reading a proper book - Nevil Shute, of course. I've come to the conclusion that the Narrow Dog (and it seems there are several Narrow Dog books) is very similar to Orbital - and that is a compliment, given that the space book is the current Booker winner. The trouble is that although they're both very well written, the Unique Selling Point seems to be endless, very clever (but somewhat repetitive) descriptions of nothing very much happening. I'm sorry, but I like something to happen.

It is this sorry search for excitement which has taken up much of the route planning: Crossing the Grand Banks by the Great Circle route would involve a course across the widest part, about 450 miles full of fog, trawlers, gas platforms etc.

Or I could opt for the Tail of the Bank - less than 200 miles, a good deal further south, so better visibility and further for the Newfoundland fishing fleet to go to run into me. No gas platforms either, as far as I can see.

But the real clincher seems to be better winds to the south, avoiding a calm in 48 hours and then giving me a slingshot on a broad reach back onto the great circle for the Fastnet.

At least, that's the plan.

*

I can't remember the last time I used gas on this boat.

I think I was in Panamarina. There had been very little wind - and Panamarina is sheltered anyway, with high ground and islands all around. There had been thick cloud for a couple of days with fairly heavy downpours. I remember harvesting gallons of freshwater caught in the awning so that I wouldn't have to run the watermaker - the water there is murky.

And I didn't have to use gas. The batteries were on something like 43% which is not low for Lithium. I could have run them down below 20% and they wouldn't have come to any harm (I could have run them flat like a mobile phone, and they wouldn't have come to any harm).

So, what I'm saying is that I didn't need to use gas - and that was months ago.

So, why am I carrying around two 7kg gas cylinders, which take up three-quarters of the space in the lazarette and could blow up the boat any time they like?

Gas is not particularly expensive, but it can be tiresome finding somewhere to get the cylinders refilled - either they don't do Butane or they don't have the right connector for a British cylinder, or - as in the Gran Canaria - gas is the responsibility of the government, so there's only one place on the whole island you can get it - right in the middle of the island, as far from all the harbours as possible. And to top it off, the law prohibits the carriage of full cylinders on any kind of public transport, including taxis. So, you have to hire a car.

No wonder I'm so enthusiastic about getting rid of the stuff.

Imagine! I could stow the storm sails in the lazarette. Just think how much space that would free up - and the drogue. All kinds of things could go in there. It might even correct the trim - she's always been down by the head.

And there's something else, since we're talking about getting rid of excess weight: The Rolls Royce gas cooker weighs an unbelievable 35kg…

At the time, nobody thought Lithium batteries in boats would take off. Lithium batteries burst into flames. Lithium batteries were stupidly expensive…

Not anymore. *Samsara's* set up is still the price of a small car, but my word, the difference it makes! I used to see by rechargeable lamps - shifting them from one conveniently placed hook to the next as I moved around the boat. Quite regularly, I would cook by the light of a head torch - desperate not to run the new AGM batteries down below 12.2V.

Now the boat's lit up like the Crystal Palace and I don't bother to turn off the Starlink - even when I go ashore. If I've anchored close enough, I can pick up the signal from the beach bar.

And, of course, I can boil a kettle in two minutes. If it's for just one cup, the inverter doesn't even bother to switch on its fan - and it doesn't heat up the whole cabin.

Best of all, by the time I've finished my cup of tea, the solar panels and the wind charger have pumped the batteries back up to where they were before I started.

So, the only decision to make is whether to just return the gas bottles to Calor but continue to cart around 35kg of redundant (and very expensive) cooker or:

1: Try and sell the cooker and buy a cheap one to replace it. This wouldn't actually be connected to anything - but it would be lighter, take up less space (meaning I could clean around it without taking all the skin of my knuckles) and it could be fixed at a lower level so I could stir a saucepan without skinning my knuckles all over again - on the deckhead.

Or 2: Spend even more money buying an electric marine cooker - that way I would get two hobs. But do I really need two hobs? And an oven - I haven't used the oven since I gave up baking bread. As for the grill: I only ever use that for toast, and an electric toaster wouldn't burn it every morning.

Of course, I do still need an oven as a Faraday cage for protecting electronics from lightning strikes - but that's just a metal box.

Maybe the thing to do is find out first if anybody will buy it. I'll put it on eBay. Then I can decide.

Day 23

Thursday 8th May 2025.
42°09.912'N 58°56.178'W.
Wind: S4. Barometer: 1025.
Day's Run: 137M.
Total: 2,834M.
Average: 123.2M.
Distance to Destination: 2,215M.

Sitting out in the cockpit with my morning coffee and my book, I couldn't believe how cold a southerly wind could be. There were occasional flashes of sunshine, but in the end, I was driven back inside. Now I am propped on the leeward berth with my flask, the logbook and the notebook. We are past the halfway mark.

The great moment passed unnoticed, just as much of the progress has passed unnoticed over the past week. Every day is pretty much the same: A smooth sea, a (cold) southerly wind blowing at Force 4 or 5 (occasionally six, as they say on the Shipping Forecast) and *Samsara* swoops along at a steady six knots.

I have a strict rule that any time I go on deck, it is in full oilskins and boots - I'm wearing so many layers that I can't afford to get any of them wet. But with the wind on the beam and a generally calm sea, there's been no spray to worry about.

So, life has developed into something of a comfortable routine - a bit of reading, a bit of writing. My two-hour Spanish lesson has had to go by the board for the last few days because

Spotify limits the amount of time you can spend listening to audiobooks, and I have to wait for this month's subscription to be paid before the clock resets. Everything should be back to normal this afternoon.

But it did mean that yesterday, I reverted to my favourite default activity: Planning future voyages. These keep changing - for no better reason than it is enormous fun thinking up new destinations. After all, what else am I going to do with all the time in the world and the whole world to spend it on...

The only bit that is set in stone is what I now call the South Atlantic Loop - leaving Gran Canaria in November just after the ARC fleet sets off (it might even be fun to leave ten minutes after them) but, instead of heading for St Lucia, I will cross the equator, call at Tristan da Cuhna, St Helena and Ascension Island before re-crossing the equator and fetching up in Grenada.

I didn't really have much of a plan after that - I mean, that's a pretty big plan in itself. But I had always promised to go and see my son George and his wife Haley in New Zealand. On the other hand, I am now rather besotted with Central America. Panama is just wonderful, but people tell me Costa Rica is just as good - and the Bay Islands in Honduras. Guatemala City ("Guate", as I am learning to call it) is one of the great capitals of the world, and Cuba will be an unforgettable experience - as long as I get there before it changes.

Just imagine how much better it would be if I could hold a proper conversation in Spanish.

The only thing stopping me has been my promise to visit George and Haley in New Zealand. The last time was when Hugo and I flew over for their wedding twelve years ago - and what a flight that was: almost 24 hours.

But then I looked at the map and saw how much shorter it would be if I went the other way, starting from Panama. As far as I can tell by looking at the Mercator projection on Navionics, it cuts off about a third of the distance.

I could leave the boat with Sylvie in Panamarina, Ramón would drive me to the airport…

Free of obligations, I began writing out a new itinerary.

Returning from Ascension in March 2026, I could make landfall in Antigua (I still haven't seen Jolly Harbour and the west of the island. Then northwest to St Kitts and Nevis, Barts and even Saba.

From there, down to Carriacou for the beginning of hurricane season, because you can't miss a chance to visit Grenada, and you can always duck down to Trinidad if anything blows up.

After that, west to Aruba because there's nothing nicer than sitting under a tree on Surfside beach and watching the sun go down over Renaissance Island - if fact there's nothing nicer than spending a day on Renaissance Island itself which you can do if you pay for a night in the marina - the same company owns both, and the hotel, and the casino - and runs a fleet of launches taking guests to spend a day with the flamingos and the second-best cocktails in the Caribbean.

And if you're in Aruba, how about dodging the shallows at the south end of the lagoon and dinner at Marina Pirata - the best seafood spaghetti outside Naples.

Next stop would be Cartagena in Colombia. This time I really would stay for a month of Spanish lessons - four hours every morning and then wander round the lanes of the Old Town having lunch and practising what I learned in the morning.

July '26 would find me back in Panama for four months in the San Blas Islands (I met a man who had been there for eight years).

Or maybe three months in the San Blas and one in Boco de Toro (even if you do have to lock up your dinghy there).

The notebook gets a bit hazy after that - but there's clearly an entry: "Nov '26 - Jun '27: Costa Rica, Honduras, Guatemala, Mexico, Cuba, Bahamas and back to Panama until November."

As I say, none of this is set in stone, but Panama has the Panama Canal, which tends to concentrate the mind on the Pacific and New Zealand. But the more I hear about the Panama Canal, the less it appeals to me.

Here are some things you might not know about a transit of the Panama Canal in a 9.7m boat.

It's going to cost upwards of $3,000.

You have to have four line-handlers, a helmsman and a pilot. That's six people (and the pilot might bring an apprentice).

The pilot must be served three meals a day (all containing meat) and supplied with unlimited bottled water. But he is taken off the boat overnight when you stop in Lake Gatun at the top (presumably, he takes his apprentice with him).

Meanwhile, the four line handlers and helmsman sleep on the boat (*Samsara* has two bunks). They all need feeding, of course.

The boat must be fitted with a holding tank capable of accommodating the effluent of six (seven?) people for two days.

In the absence of a holding tank, a Porta-Potti may be hired (they're joking, of course).

All of this is preceded by up to a month's stay in Shelter Bay Marina while you engage an agent, hire long lines and huge fenders and complete the famously extensive Panamanian paperwork.

But if you want to get to the Pacific, there's no alternative.

Except there is.

How would it be at the end of the hurricane season in the San Blas - November 2027 - if I were to head north and spend six months really getting to know the Bahamas - the Bahamian cruising permit is not cheap, but it is valid for six months.

Then in May, I could head east to the Canaries again but since I wouldn't be aiming for the Caribbean, I wouldn't have to wait for November, I could set off down into the South Atlantic straight away - just as soon as I'd stocked the boat at Dino's Supermarket - and this time, not stopping: South of the Cape of Good Hope, across the Indian Ocean, South of Australia and landfall in South Island New Zealand.

If I break something and need to put in somewhere, there's always Cape Town or Freemantle, but wouldn't that be an adventure?

Wouldn't that make a book?

But, like I said, plans are written in sand.

Or does seeing it on the screen here count as stone?

Meanwhile, when I get to the Isle of Man, I'm going to have to find some way of stowing the spinnaker poles that doesn't involve flimsy plastic brackets on the guardrails. From what I hear of the seas in the Indian Ocean, anything stowed on deck must be considered dispensable. I'm going to have to find some way of emptying the cockpit faster, too.

These are the sorts of things that come to mind when sailing across a calm sea in a steady wind. Maybe it's wearing three layers that does it.

Day 24

Friday 9th May 2025.
42°30.930'N 56°27.782'W.
Wind: S4. Barometer: 1026.
Day's Run: 112M.
Total: 2,946M.
Average: 122.7M.
Distance to Destination: 2,103M.

I'm not sure that Starlink is helping make this the most exciting book.

A feature of The Voyage #1 & #2 was the fact that I had no long-range communications - no weather forecasts. No contact with the shore. No news (I didn't know Boris Johnson had gone). This time, even though I am not opening news apps, I couldn't avoid the Pope dying - and the new one being an American.

But more significantly, I am not now going to cross the Grand Banks - which I would undoubtedly have done without Starlink. It is, after all, the most direct route which, on the face of it, would get me there faster.

However, the day before yesterday, a huge area of calm showed up on the 48-hour forecast - right on my track. I used to think that offshore weather forecasts were all very well for big boats and multihulls which could outrun weather systems, but not much good if your average speed is five knots. But I'm not sure that is any longer the case.

Forecasting over 48 hours - even 72 hours - is now so precise that I have the option to alter course by 20° and carry the wind right past the calm by keeping to the south. The new route would take me across the Tail of the Bank rather than the widest part. It would also, of course, keep me away from the gas platforms, and I would only have to worry about fishing boats for 150 miles instead of 300.

But then I saw I can expect winds of up to 30kts on Sunday night and Monday morning - just when I would have been crossing from the 2000m contour to the 100m in the space of 25 miles. That is like the Bay of Biscay: When a gale piles up on a gradient like that, you end up with some of the roughest conditions found anywhere in the world. It's just not sensible.

I thought about it all night and, this morning, went out and tweaked the starboard rein of the Aries three times. Each click is 6°. Three clicks, 18° (the nearest I can get to 20°). We are now heading due east, directly for the Tail of the Bank buoy 330 miles away. We should reach it in the early hours of Monday morning - just as the wind hits.

With any luck, it will be really boring.

If you want to know why I didn't get up in the night to change course, the reason is fairly simple. It was 11°C in the cabin. The water temperature was 8°C. I was zipped into the heavy-duty sleeping bag (4°C-17°C) and wearing extra-thick thermal socks. I had the draught excluder pulled tight round my shoulders and the hood up (over a woolly hat). If there had been an emergency, it would have taken me five minutes to get out - and a change of course was not an emergency.

I can hardly believe that three weeks ago I was lying on the top of the lightweight sleeping bag, wearing no clothes at all and with the fan running all night. People are going to ask me: "Are you mad?"

I'm not sure what I'm going to say.

Well, there's a bit of good news. I unscrewed the section of the cabin sole that covers the watermaker pump and the 5-micron filter - the starboard cockpit locker was full of gash bags and recycling, and I wanted to get it out of the way. What should I find down there but a 12-pack of beer!

I don't think there's any danger of running out now. If I can keep up this average, I'll reach Douglas IOM in three weeks.

This is what you get for buying another two 12-packs every time you pass the little shop by the fuel dock - beer is that cheap in Panama.

Mind you, I'm still looking forward to a Guinness in Dublin…

In fact, if it really is going to be only three weeks, I don't have to eat rice with bugs in it any more. Didn't I calculate that I could last for 20 days on the noodles, spaghetti and mashed potato?

Then there are the bean sprouts. They're growing very slowly in this cold, but they seem to be managing. I have a huge bottle of honey and mustard dressing (I think it's a typically American half-gallon). I am beginning to hanker after tomatoes, though - and dreaming of eating out. When I arrive, I shall go out for my first three meals (and that includes lunch).

On other fronts, I have finished Nevil Shute's *Most Secret*. I think it took two days - but that's what you get with a book in which something actually happens. With some trepidation, I have started Daphne du Maurier's Rebecca. I've never read it and somehow feel I ought to. The trepidation is because I remember Jamaica Inn from years ago and not thinking much of it.

It happens if you're a philistine. But I do need something to occupy myself. It's too cold to sit in the cockpit and watch the sea, and playing the Clarinet with one duff key is just plain frustrating. I tried to remember that every time I pressed it with the little finger of my left hand, I would have to find an opportunity to flick it up again before the next time. That sort of thing plays havoc with *Old Stack O'Lee Blues*.

*

Well, I know I'm back in the Temperate Zone. It's foggy and raining. I don't know what the temperature is out there, but it's only 14°C in the cabin, and the water is down to 9.3°C. Because we're now in single digits, there's room for a + sign, just in case there was any doubt.

It's becoming rather obvious why people spend years in the San Blas.

Not for me, though. Not with my little boredom problem.

The latest excitement is that the rope clutch for the first reef pennant is slipping again, even though I end-for-ended the line. I can think of two solutions: Replace the 8mm line with 10mm, but I'm not sure I have a spare that's long enough. I can't take it off and measure it at the moment because I've got the reef in (tied down to a cleat on the mast). I could use the port sheet of the Super Zero, but then I wouldn't be able to use that for the sail, at least not on starboard tack.

Now, there's a thought - but if you start chasing it, you end up tacking the sail by swapping the single sheet from one side to the other!

The second option is to tighten the clutch. Can you tighten a rope clutch? Are they made to be adjusted? I've no idea. I'll ask Google...

What it is to have communications - but, on the other hand, isn't that taking something away from the whole point of a long-distance singlehanded voyage?

Think of Robin Knox Johnston in 1968, taking all day to make contact with a shore station - and then hurrying to pass his message before the signal faded. He didn't have time to ask how to fix stuff. But then, as a Master Mariner trained in the British Merchant Navy of the 1950s, there wasn't much on Suhaili that he couldn't fix. If you want to learn about real self-sufficiency, read *A World of My Own* - the bit where he shoots a shark so he can dive under the boat and re-caulk the hull.

But, for a minute there, I thought I might be back in the old days. Suddenly, my phone screen announced that an update was available for Starlink. Well, since it appeared that I had already downloaded it, all I needed to do was approve the installation - and yes, I did wonder whether Elon Musk had charged his usual £1.86/GB rate for his own download. Anyway, I clicked "Yes".

Immediately the screen announced that I had to sign in again - although, of course, now I couldn't because I was trying to use the system to access the system! Meanwhile, "the system" assumed I had some other access to the internet - wifi or mobile data at the very least.

Of course, I hadn't. I was stuffed! This was the Spotify problem all over again (it needs to check once a month that you've paid the subscription or it shuts down and you get no more music for six weeks except the same 20 "classic driving anthems" you downloaded for emergencies.)

I was looking at three weeks and 2,000 miles with no weather forecasts, no email - no advice on how to adjust rope clutches. I would have to ask a ship to send a message to Tamsin saying that I hadn't sunk.

Although, interestingly, it seems that the PolarSteps tracker would still have kept advancing five minutes at a time. That can't be right, surely?

*

No wonder it's light at four o'clock in the morning. I haven't been adjusting the clocks. I thought my phone would do it but, apparently only when it connects to a mobile signal (even if I don't activate mobile data). When I did, the time jumped forward by an hour. However, here I am three days past the 60°W longitude and I'm still on Havana time (82°W).

Think about it: There are 360° of longitude and 24 hours in the day. $360 \div 24 = 15$. Ergo, 15° of longitude accounts for one hour.

On Thursday I crossed 60°, so $60 \div 15$ is 4. I should be four hours behind Greenwich. It's not 11:15. It's 12:15.

I've missed the midday log entry. Hell, I'm late for the lunchtime beer…

Day 25

> Saturday 10th May 2025.
> 42°26.808'N 53°29.868'W.
> Wind: S4. Barometer: 1024.
> Day's Run: 13124
> Total: 3,077M.
> Average: 123.1M.
> Distance to Destination:1,972.
> ETA: 16 days - May 26th.

How about that? Close enough to start thinking about estimated times of arrival - and May 26th is the *first* day of the TT!

Mind you, a word about the calculation: All I do is take the "Distance to destination" and divide it by the latest "Average day's run". So, this could change dramatically with a few days of calm. Meanwhile, it's great for morale.

I looked up slipping rope clutches and came up with all sorts of complicated instructions for replacing worn clutch plates. Then there were lessons on how to insert a replacement core into the worn section of line - and everyone knows you can't work with braided rope when it's been out in the wind and weather for a few months.

Then there was the obvious solution: Replace the line.

What I did was try some experiments on other sections of line and came to the conclusion that if I could just shift the load six inches one way or the other, it would hold. I did this by moving the stopper knot at the mast to the very end of the pennant, then centred the boom and stood up on the cockpit seats and pulled more rope through the block and took up the slack by doubling the line when I tied it off.

We shall see if it works because today's forecast is still offering a gale on Monday - although the glass is still way up at 1024. It's going to have to start dropping soon if there really is any unpleasantness heading this way. Meanwhile, I now have only 170 miles to go to the waypoint off the Tail of the Bank. I should be clear before the wind arrives.

And that's the last waypoint before the Fastnet.

Isn't it the strangest thing to wake up in a dream and not realise that you haven't woken up at all but have just woken up in the dream - that you've actually dreamed that you woke up? And reality gets all twisted?

I was back at the Daily Mail in the days when they had old black Bakelite telephones (I was never there when they had old black Bakelite telephones). All the same, it must have been about 1977. I was relatively new and just beginning to get myself noticed.

David English, the legendary editor who had appointed me in the first place, stared at me from the back bench. For some reason, I was sitting right up against it, whereas everybody knows that's where the sub-editors sit.

He spoke. He said: "Give it to Passmore. See what he makes of it. The night news editor, a ginger-haired man with half-moon spectacles on the end of a long nose (I'm sure his name will come to me, although what he was doing there in the daytime, I have no idea), said: "Are you sure, he's very new …something as big as this…"

English pursed his lips the way important executives do when making important executive decisions - and the night desk reporter brought me the press release (the night news editor only ever rose to his feet to go and drink Brakspear's at the City Snooker Club.)

The job was written on parchment in old gothic script with illuminated capitals. It was some sort of complicated and important story. It seemed there was a big international conference in London. Today was the conclusion.

I rolled two sheets of copy paper into the stand-up-and-beg Imperial typewriter (in fact we had modern grey Olympias - the Imperials belonged in local papers with no money for new technology).

The way it was done in those days was to type on two sheets of copy paper with a thick, waxy sheet of double-sided carbon between them. This ensured that the type appeared on both sides of the top sheet, which could then be fed into a Roneo machine and turned into 13 copies. These were distributed all over the building by dozens of cheeky teenage messengers from London's East End, all of them sons of the printers - the closed shop saw to that.

I had a lot of trouble with my diplomatic story. I worked on it all day - didn't take lunch. Other people's empty canteen plates piled up on the other side of the desk. Then someone would throw a newspaper on the top of them so that they would lie in ambush for any unwary hack who wasn't expecting to be confronted by a half sausage or a mess of congealed liver and mashed potato.

Somewhere around four o'clock (rather late), I typed "ends" on the bottom of my copy and - trying my best to be unobtrusive - slipped it into the wire tray where it was snatched away immediately, duplicated in an instant and delivered at top speed to the copy taster, the lawyer, the editor, and all those other important executives with functions I could only guess at.

I sat and thought that I hadn't made a very good job of it.

Ten minutes later, Neville Hodgkinson was at my side. Neville was the medical correspondent and a really nice guy. We all felt for him when his wife wrote a piece in the Femail pages saying how liberating it was that she and her husband had agreed to give up sex. Nobody was quite sure how much of a mutual decision this had been.

Anyway, in the dream, Neville was the diplomatic correspondent (not John Dickie, *see above*).

Neville had my copy in his hand and leaned over, conspiratorially: "Look, you can't go with this. It won't do at all. For one thing, it's far too short - and where's the colour? That's why they gave it to you. It looks as though you didn't even go to the press conference."

I didn't.

"You weren't there? That won't do. Look, do it again before they ask. Make it at least look as though you were there…"

And he began dictating - bags of description: The room (he was there for press conferences every week). The people involved (he knew them all).

I typed as fast as I could - so that the type bars got all tangled up in a sort of metallic fist, nowhere near the paper, and had to be picked apart.

At one point, Neville dictated: "Mozambique, China (Taiwan), Angola…"

I typed "Mozambique, China, Taiwan…"

"No, no. Not China *and* Taiwan. Peking claims Taiwan as its own (he called it Peking).

It took us a while to get that sorted out.

I really don't know how it ended up - which version they printed… or maybe neither… because suddenly I wasn't miserably ham-fisted in the newsroom watching David English's confused and disappointed expression and wondering whether I was going to keep my job - or, worse, be relegated to the graveyard shift of 2.00a.m. to 10.00a.m.

Because, suddenly I wasn't in the newsroom any more. I was sailing off the Grand Banks of Newfoundland, and nobody was looking to see if I did it right, and nobody was telling me I wasn't, because there was no doubt in my mind that I was doing it exactly right.

Despite there being nothing in the Windy "currents" chart about the Gulf Stream flowing this far north, *Samsara* was rattling along at nine knots over the ground (10.2 at one point). Naturally, this would be impossible under my own steam, even though I did have 20kts of wind on the beam. There must be some current helping me. All that water was moving northeast and suddenly found its way blocked by what was effectively a mountain range rising from the ocean floor at 4000m to a peak of just 100m. What is all that water going to do? It's like the wind blowing through the Canary Islands and producing "acceleration zones" between them. The only difference was that this was below the surface.

Anyway, it seemed I had taken the right decision to go south. The increased speed would more than make up for the extra distance - quite apart from avoiding the fishing boats, gas platforms, fog and rough seas due when the gale arrived on Monday.

It was quite some time before I woke up - or at least realised I was already awake - with a feeling of great satisfaction and self-confidence.

How did I know it was not to last…

Day 26

Sunday 11th May 2025
. 42°32.129'N 50°13.939'W.
Wind: S5. Barometer 1015.
Day's Run: 145M.
Total: 3,222M.
Average: 123.9M.
Distance to Destination:1,868M.
ETA: 15 days = 26th May.

Now past the Tail of the Bank, I could turn north onto the Great Circle route for the Fastnet - and I could recalculate the distance. Until now, steering for a succession of waypoints, I had simply deducted the day's run from the previous day's "Distance to destination". Now the plotter would tell me the Great Circle distance, and I could just add the 277 miles for getting round the corner and up the Irish Sea.

But now I came to look at the chart, I realised quite how far up the Irish Sea I would have to sail to get to the Isle of Man. It was practically in Scotland.

Would it be a shorter distance if I went round the north of Ireland instead?

Certainly, it would be - by 131 miles. More than a day, given the stupendous average daily mileage delivered by the Gulf Stream.

I plotted a waypoint three miles north of a tiny island off the Ulster coast called Inishtrahull, 1,825 miles away. From there, it was only another 143M to Douglas. According to the current daily average, that would get us there by the day of the start of the TT - with two whole weeks of thrills, including "Mad Sunday" when anyone on any old bike can ride the course at any daft speed they like.

I went up and gybed onto the new course.

It was while I was doing this that I noticed just how cold it was. I don't have an outside thermometer but, while I was getting out the spinnaker pole, the light piston release line came undone and I had the devil's own job retying it with frozen fingers. When I got back to the cockpit, I saw the sea temperature was down to 3.5°C. That was bad news

The lower the sea temperature, the more chance there is of ice.

The new course did keep me south of the "Southern Iceberg Limit", but icebergs are notoriously bad at checking their limits. Suddenly, I didn't feel so good anymore. I checked to see what difference it would make if I were to revert to the Fastnet - but quite frankly, the difference was negligible at this end of the track, and once I got past the southern point of Greenland, I would be out of the path of the Labrador Current, which is what brings them south in the first place. The only thing wrong with this theory is that the waypoint south of Greenland is still 500 miles away.

I checked the Internet and found a site which told me the Active Iceberg Season ends in May (but did not specify the beginning or the end). Another insisted that at this time of year, bergs had been spotted as far south as 39°N. That's ridiculous. That's the latitude of Lisbon.

I switched on the radar and set a guard zone of between one and three miles ahead. I don't have much confidence in it - partly because I have to read the instructions every time I switch it on, and also because it's an old black-and-white model with an LCD screen and beeps so often I end up ignoring it. Anyway, it would only pick up something big enough to sink the Titanic. Something capable of sinking me would be, as they say, below the radar - and I didn't give much for my chances in water of 3.5°C. I was thinking of that as I made my way forward to pole out the headsail.

I took to scanning the horizon. The horizon was less than half a mile away in the fog.

And so, I came below again, peeled off the outerwear, pulled on a thick sweater and made a cup of tea with about a dessert spoonful of honey in it. Then I had to use a knife to chip at the Nutella jar.

We'll see how things look in 500 miles.

*

Conditions are about as unpleasant as any I can remember. I have 8kts of following wind, but such a huge and irregular sea that it shakes all the wind out of the sails. Visibility is about two wave-lengths, the sea temperature is down to 3.3°C, and we're making less than 3kts.

Below, it is cold and damp and I just got taken unawares by a violent roll and shot across the cabin to smash a locker door - broke all the facing off it and the catch as well, so that I've had to redistribute most of what was stowed there and wedge it shut with cocktail sticks.

To cheer myself up, I decided on a hot lunch (it was four o'clock). Amazingly, in the soup container I found - as well as the awful Dominican Republic brew - two proper Cup-a-Soups (curry flavour with Dutch instructions), and a genuine British Batchelor's Potato and Leak. The packet felt suspiciously solid, but the best-before date was April 2025, so I reconstituted it in an insulated mug and added a Maggi cube (there really isn't much that can't be improved by the addition of a Maggi cube).

I ate it with a spoon, adding tostadas to give it some body. I'm not sure it tasted much of potato and leek, but at least it was hot.

*

It is seven degrees in the cabin. I am like one of those little old men you read about - surviving on a state pension and having to choose between heating and eating. I have been in bed all morning. Wearing all my clothes.

This has been going on for days. Last night we were going so slowly I turned off the radar, reasoning that if we hit anything, it would be so gently, I might not notice.

Certainly, I didn't notice that we had gybed and when I got up at 0430, I discovered the preventer had been chafing on the shroud for hours. It was so cold - the water temperature is now 2.9°C - that once I'd got the basic stuff sorted out, I came down and made a determined search for the neoprene gloves (found them eventually - and another two rolls of kitchen paper).

Next thing I know, it's 0530 and no warmer. Everything is grey and clammy. At least the sea has gone down - but that just gives the impression that the wind will never blow again. And yet it does - just enough to move us at a knot or two.

I went down again and found the thermometer had moved up to 8°C - whoopee! That must be due to my body heat! I believe a human being give off 1kW.

I got back into bed and put the clocks forward by another hour. It will be days before we reach 45°W but it's ridiculous being this light so early.

It did entitle me to breakfast. The Gulf Stream Breakfast has a freezing point of 8°C, apparently - and it took two hands to squeeze the runny honey bottle.

I can't understand it, I should be clear of the Labrador Current by now. I've plotted a position on the chart due south of Greenland at which I can expect the warm North Atlantic Current to kick in. This is the one that washes bits of coral onto Hebridean beaches.

It is still 258 miles away.

I'm going back to bed - to dream of the Dutch curry-flavoured Cup-a-Soup.

Somebody should start a charity for me.

Day 27

Monday 12th May 2025.
43°04.3240'N 48°40.996'W.
Wind: W5. Barometer: 1014.
Day's Run: 73M.
Total: 3,295M.
Average: 122M.
Distance to Destination: 1,899M.
ETA: 15.6 days = May 27th

How about that? It turns out it is worth complaining about the weather after all.

I had fallen asleep in bed - because that's what you do in bed, even though I was supposed to be listening to my *Spanish Language Builder* audiobook - and woke to find us gybed again.

Only this time it was in bright sunshine. Honestly, there was not a cloud in the sky and a steady 15kt wind blowing out of the west. The sea temperature, suddenly, had leapt to 6.1°C.

It was still cold - still only 8°C in the cabin but somehow it didn't seem so unpleasant. Settled on a broad reach, with the wind puffing up to 25kts, *Samsara* was skidding all over the ocean. I did consider trailing warps - they were still heaped up in the cockpit from last time. But if this really was going to be the fringes of a gale - and that's what the Windy map suggested - it was far better to hand the main and let her carry on being led by the nose with a bigger headsail.

It was while I was doing this that I discovered the chafe on the top of the main halyard. This was new, about 20cm below the shackle. I shall have to end-for-end it when I get in. I'm not going up the mast out here. If the worst comes to the worst and it chafes through, I can use the topping lift.

And so eventually I came below again to find we were making almost the same speed as before - and a lot more comfortably. Without the main forcing her up to windward and then the Aries over-correcting and slamming us the other way, life below is no worse than a slightly-rolly anchorage (better in fact than Pasito Blanco in an easterly).

I treated myself to lunch - a hot lunch of the second packet of Dominican Republic dehydrated soup. Making it according to the instructions improved it marginally, but it still tasted as if the main ingredient was monosodium glutamate. I rounded it off with chunks of Nutella (Nutella comes in chunks below 10°C. Just dig around with a knife and shake them out.)

I plan to enjoy this new lifestyle while I can. It's not going to last. My clever plan to go north is now going to reward me with a couple of days of calms at the end of the week and then about five days of headwinds. It could be worse. If I had taken the southern route, I would be due for a 45kt gale somewhere north west of the Azores - and driving me down onto them, as well. I think "small mercies" is the phrase…

*

Five degrees in the cabin when I woke up this morning. Maybe that was because I was keeping all the body heat I was generating in the sleeping bag with me. I would have two, one inside the other, but the zips are broken on both the lightweight ones. Sleeping bags haven't been much of a priority over the past year or so. I hate to say it, but I must be getting used to this.

From time to time, I look wistfully at the heater - no help there because I haven't any charcoal - didn't think I'd need it.

Part of the big refit was going to be a diesel heater - I could light that any time I liked, but I would still be limited by my 50-litre diesel tank. Anyway, it was going to cost a fortune, and at that time I thought I was headed for the sunshine…

Outside, the wind was down to 16kts. When it was still at 16kts after breakfast, it seemed sensible to switch back to the Aries - I'd been on the electric autopilot all night because the wind strength kept fluctuating, and the electronic sensor can keep track of the rudder loading.

The trouble was that the Aries didn't seem able to cope at all, even with a steady wind: Within a couple of minutes, we were beam on. I adjusted it - and adjusted it again.

It was quite some time before I realised the tiller lines weren't moving. The thing wasn't working at all. I went and inspected it. The servo paddle was trailing along behind at the end of its safety line. The sacrificial link had broken. Obviously, it had hit something. That happens from time to time in coastal waters when it may run over a lobster pot (or I back it into an underwater obstruction, as happened on the slip in Aruba). But out here, what was there for it to run into? Did I really come that close to an iceberg?

Obviously, I needed to recover it, but these were far from ideal conditions. There was a big sea running, and the boat was being thrown all over the place - but, on the other hand, leaving the paddle trailing along behind was just asking for trouble. If the line chafed through, that would be the end of it until I could get another sent from Amsterdam.

Actually, that wasn't such a bad idea. Lean Nelis, the Dutch plumber who bought the Aries moulds (and therefore, effectively the brand), changed the position of the bolts.

Only after I had taken delivery of three new ones did I realise the holes didn't line up. I took them to a machine show and, with a lot of trial and error, bodged together a solution.

Or so it seemed.

Meanwhile, there I was, balancing on the back of the boat with the wind gusting to 25kts. It was all right really. I was drifting under bare poles. If I fell over, the boat was only doing a knot. I could swim that fast.

I glanced at the water temperature: 7°C. Maybe best not to fall in.

With the utmost care, I removed the windvane assembly and turned the main frame upside down on its mounting (you can do that with the lift-up version). Now I could get at everything - I've done it before this way.

Correction, I've done it before this way in calm weather with everything fitting together like a jigsaw for the under-sevens.

This time, the bolt for the servo-paddle had to be coaxed in with the big hammer (so, maybe the correct analogy is a 1,000-piece jigsaw - one that lives on the dining room table until Twelfth Night).

So far, so good. The sleeve slipped neatly onto the main shaft. I was now working over the back of the boat, so it seemed a good idea to tie the spanner to the end of the 4mm line used to adjust the course - what I call the reins, imagining I am carriage driving. By the way, I often wondered what the rings on the ends of spanners were for. I never use them for tightening nuts.

Of course! They're for attaching a piece of string if you happen to be using the spanner while hanging off the back of a boat.

The sacrificial link slipped home onto the main shaft - the servo paddle sticking up at an angle. This is a tricky operation. It is not really practical to tie a safety line onto a bolt. That is why I carry a spare. All the same…

I held the bolt very carefully while I plied the spanner - grateful for my neoprene gloves in such a delicate operation.

This didn't seem to get us anywhere

I withdrew the bolt and found that, by the merest sliver of a millimetre, the holes didn't line up.

OK, so we can fix that. I went and fetched my little B&Q rechargeable electric drill. Of course, the bit jammed straight away - and, straight away, as soon as I reversed the drill to free it, the chuck loosened (because it doesn't have a proper chuck key) and as soon as I withdrew the drill, the bit fell out and into the Newfoundland Basin, which is what they call 4,000 metres of water round here.

So, I tried the big hammer instead.

The reason that didn't work was because there just wasn't enough room for both the bolt and the index fingertip of a left-hand neoprene glove - and since it was my hand in the glove, I was now as securely attached to the boat as if I really had worn a harness after all.

Actually, I was attached a bit more precisely than that. I couldn't even get as far as the cockpit - where I had put the spanner which might, with luck, release the neoprene fingertip.

The only thing to do was get the hand out of the glove. Believe me, it is easier to replace the sacrificial sleeve on an Aries servo paddle than get a wet hand out of a wet neoprene glove while trying to hold on with the other hand when you can't get your teeth close enough without falling over (in which case, why not use the other hand)

Which is what I did.

It was somewhere around this point that I took a good look at the sea and realised it was a lot rougher than it had been when I started - not surprising, seeing that the wind had now risen to a steady 25kts.

It wasn't as if it was that urgent - the autopilot could cope in the meantime. I stowed the windvane assembly and the servo paddle, lashed the main frame upside down and went and looked at the weather forecast. Apparently, I'm due for a calm late this afternoon - and I still have my bolt!

Day 28

Tuesday 13th May 2025.
44°15.368'N 46°10.253'W.
Wind: W5. Barometer: 1018.
Day's. run: 130M.
Total: 3,425M.
Average: 122.3M.
Distance to Destination: 1,770M.
ETA: 14.5 days = May 28th

The calm did arrive - well, not a complete calm, but by 3.30, the wind was down to 10kts and I set about removing the main frame. I coiled the control lines, leaving just one attached in case I dropped the whole thing, stood up on the aft deck, reached down until I was bent double over the pushpit - and lifted it off.

The hard part was manoeuvring it down into the cabin, holding it with both hands, which left none for holding on.

Then we had an hour and a half with the jigsaw puzzle. The trouble was that each of the sacrificial sleeves had twelve holes in it - the original four which would fit my new shaft and a modern paddle. But my paddle dated from the 1980s, so the machine shop in Aruba to drill another four, which turned out to be in the wrong places - so then I went back for a further four. By this time you could argue there were more holes than metal, so it was probably best to stop.

Even so, anything that fitted the shaft didn't fit the paddle - and when I started with the paddle, I couldn't get the holes to line up on the shaft.

I couldn't drill it out with my "Little Carpenter's Electric Drill Kit" because I'd lost the 10mm drill bit. But I could, it occurred to me in a flash of inspiration, use a thinner bolt. There was only the tiniest trace of the dark grey of the shaft showing at the bottom of the hole. Would it be possible to cut a new thread? It was a steel bolt into aluminium after all.

I carry a spare bolt, so it was brand new with a sharp thread. Ideally, it should be one with a hexagonal head for a spanner, but all I had been able to find at the time was a "machine screw" with a head for a screwdriver - the big screwdriver, with the hexagonal shaft.

Here's a tip: make sure your big screwdriver has a hexagonal shaft - so you can get an 8mm spanner on it for purchase. If you do that, you will find you can cut a new thread into cast aluminium.

It is only now, editing this in retrospect, that I remember I have a round file, tapered to a point certainly smaller than a 10mm hole. I'll keep that in reserve for next time - I just hope there never is a next time.

The second hole presented a much bigger problem - almost half the hole was blocked. Think about it: Almost half of 10mm is 4mm - which leaves 6mm clear for a 6mm machine screw. It stuck out a good bit on the other side, but I wasn't about to start cutting it off for the sake of appearances.

All I had to do now was put the whole thing back on the stern.

This was a bit more of a proposition this time. The frame without the paddle had been heavy enough. Now with the whole thing assembled, it must have weighed 25kg. I tied a sheet around my waist just in case - although a glance at the cockpit instruments showed the water temperature at 7.4°C, so I wouldn't have given myself much chance of climbing back on. I would worry about that once I was in the water…

It took several attempts to get the thing slotted into place. On a couple of occasions, I just had to rest - and of course I couldn't let go of it and have a lie down for five minutes. I took my breather head down, doubled over the pushpit. I really must start doing some exercises. When you get old, your muscles waste away if you're not manhandling self-steering gear on a daily basis.

But eventually, persistence will always win the day, and I had the thing in place upside down. Now all I had to do was let it drop into its correct attitude and do up the bolts - job done.

Except, now that I thought about it, there was something odd about the paddle sticking up there above my head. I'm very used to it like that because that's the way I stow it in harbour - but then it points the other way…

I'd only put it on back to front.

I recognise that I do have a problem with orientation - things being both upside down and back to front (see the abandoning ship chapter in the *Old Man Sailing* book - a story repeated in *Faster, Louder, Riskier, Sexier*. Fortunately, it was a simple matter to withdraw the 6mm machine screw, twiddle the paddle through 180° and do it up again.

Meanwhile, I should mention that we were still sailing under autopilot - doing a good five knots through the water. Now I had to turn the gear the right way up, but the paddle, which gets its power from the flow of water passing over it, flatly refused to allow the mere weight of aluminium (even 25kg) to interfere with the job in hand.

In short, I had to stop the boat.

But I couldn't let go of the Aries. It was ridiculous; all I needed was someone to lift the steering ram off the tiller and give it a push to bring the boat up into the wind - but this is exactly the problem when you don't have a crew. In the end, I gave the job to my left foot.

With a bit of stretching, it managed to knock the ram off its peg and force the helm across. In no time at all, sails were flapping and the bubbles at the stern were going sideways. Seizing the opportunity before she swung off the wind and attempted to go sailing again, I rammed both bolts home. We were back in business!

Except we weren't. No matter what I did with the vane orientation, the paddle stayed resolutely at the far end of its travel to port, and the control lines didn't move an inch (which meant, nor did the tiller).

The whole kit and caboodle had to come back up again while I twiddled and peered and experimented and tried to find out what was wrong.

Two things became clear: Choosing either of the other two holes in the paddle wouldn't solve it, and I wouldn't be able to undo the newly-cut shaft fastening without taking it all below again.

I was just thinking I didn't fancy that (and then chastising myself for being a wimp) when I noticed something else. The paddle would turn further in one direction than the other. That couldn't be right, surely - and it meant that even if I did solve the problem with the bolts, it was never going to work properly anyway. Perhaps it was something to do with the shaft being bent.

Anyway, it was now 6.15 - past the hour of the beer - and the cabin was still a mess of toolboxes, discarded bolts, drill bits and spanners. One of the toolboxes had helped by emptying itself all over the floor.

Solemnly, I cleared it all up, stowed the paddle and the wind vane assembly, returned the main frame to its proper position - the useless sacrificial sleeve dragging in the water - settled the boat on her proper course with sails nicely trimmed and went below to peel off my oilskins and collect *two* cans of beer from the focsle. Interestingly, I don't store them in the fridge any more. The fridge is set at 12°C, but the air temperature is 10°C. I use a neoprene "beer cosy", common in the tropics for keeping the beer cold, Now it's for stopping my hand getting cold.

I took the beer out into the cockpit. Now, there's a surprise - when was the last time I did that? But the seats were dry. The sky was a deep blue and winding up for a fabulous sunset. I got myself settled on the lee side facing the sun with a bowl of peanuts (OK, so we'll run out before we get there, but I deserved a treat - why did you think I had two beers lined up?)

And I had the Kindle with *Rebecca* as soon as I opened the cover. What a fantastic writer is Daphne du Maurier - and this is her crowning achievement. I'm such a philistine…

But I didn't read it. Instead, I kept watching the waves. I hadn't realised quite how big they were. Obviously, I had other things on my mind. But, they were up level with the top of the guardrails when they were less than a boat's length away. I was sure one of them was going to break straight into the cockpit and all over me. Never mind me. It would wash all the peanuts out of the bowl. I kept watching, tempting fate…

It didn't last. I wasn't enjoying the sunset. I wasn't reading my book. I was just waiting to get soaked. I came down again and set up at my usual table - on the lee berth, feet up on the windward (three cushions behind me, so my feet will reach that far), my pillow beside me to stop the peanut bowl from sliding off…

*

I have never given a name to the electronic autopilot - come to that, I have never given a name to the Aries. People usually give their self-steering a name - it is, after all, like having an extra crew member. The ancient and tattered sheet of instructions that came with my gear 40 years ago even suggests that new owners should give careful thought to a name, along with the advice that "if it moves, oil it."

I did try once, I called it "Arnold" - it seems I call everything "Arnold" - but the name never stuck. I suppose I am just too unsentimental. "The Aries", it remained.

But after a night with the Raytheon electronic autopilot in charge, I was beginning to feel a real affection for it - after all, we have 1,600 miles to go - pretty much a whole Atlantic crossing at these latitudes, and I'm going to be relying on it to steer for 24 hours a day in all conditions for at least two weeks. In other words, more than 300 hours non-stop.

Until now, I've only used it for getting in and out of harbours while I walk around the decks organising warps and fenders and anchors - putting on sail ties and so on. It's good at that.

Also, it's good at steering the boat in very light winds when the Aries is not at its best. Indeed, I would have been quite happy with the old cheapo TillerPilot - but that packed up every time it rained. I was spending so much on replacing circuit boards that it made sense to go for the more expensive model, which keeps its brain in the engine bay.

Isn't there something in the Hitch-hiker's Guide to the Galaxy about never trusting a life form unless you can see where it keeps its brain?

Dave Jones, who fitted it in Conwy, just called it "modular".

Some people rely on these things all the time. Most long-term cruisers carry their dinghy in davits across the stern, which creates problems for a windvane. The owner of a big Amel once showed me how he could swap his autopilot for the spare in two minutes (without tools!)

Maybe these things aren't so flimsy after all. After a night of faultlessly following the compass course, I'm beginning to appreciate mine.

Of course, you do have to manage the sail area rather more carefully - a massive mechanical device like an Aries - 25kg of cast aluminium and Dyneema will control a boat even though she might be over-pressed.

Microchips - or more exactly, the length of the arm of the drive unit - just can't cope with that.

Look at it this way: I haven't seen a ship for ten days. The radar guard zone is supposed to be taking care of icebergs. Theoretically, I can sleep for as long as I like. But with the Aries, I would set an alarm every 90 minutes. If the wind changed - and the course with it - I could spend hours going in the wrong direction.

With the autopilot set to follow the compass, I'll soon know if the ship needs me - flapping sails or waves crashing over the deck make an excellent alarm clock. Getting thrown out of bed thanks to an unexpected gybe works quite well, too.

So, unbidden - without any deliberate decision - it suddenly came into my head that the autopilot was called "Eric". Really, it was as sudden as that - as though one of the under-gardeners in Rebecca had rendered some vital service to the heroine (so clever that she is never named) and consequently he is rewarded a recognisable identity.

We shall see if it sticks. Meanwhile, the note of the wind charger has dropped, telling me that maybe it's time to shake out that reef... no, it's back to a steady moan. I'm OK for a bit.

"Eric", meanwhile, has compensated for the change in weather helm - I imagine him taking a foot off the lee cockpit seat and straightening up, taking one hand off the tiller to reach into the pocket of his oilskin for pipe and tobacco...

Yes, Eric is in his late 50s, as a young man he crewed on the 12metres in the grand old days of Sir Thomas Lipton and Shamrock. Eric has a clasp knife and an earring. Given a bit more familiarity, he may have some old yarns to pass along.

I'll let you know.

*

Since we're celebrating, I decided it was high time for some heat in the cabin. At least with the slightly higher water temperature and the sunshine, it was up to 10°C below, but that's still not what I would call "cosy".

When I had gas cooking, all I had to do was boil a kettle, and in the ten minutes it took, with most of the heat escaping around the bottom of the kettle, the cabin could get quite toasty. The induction hob is far too efficient for that - which is quite a good thing when the cabin starts off at 32°C. Not so good now, though.

If I really am going to give the Calor cylinders back to the chandlery in Falmouth and claim my deposit, maybe I should give them back empty. In other words, maybe I should be using up the last of the gas now.

So, the little induction hob is back in the locker under the focsle berth, and we're back on gas - and the cabin is deliciously warm, even though I'm still waiting for my cup of tea.

Day 29

> Wednesday 14th May 2025.
> 45°25.934'N 43°56.338'W.
> Wind NW5. Barometer: 1013.
> Day's Run: 119M.
> Total: 3,544M.
> Average: 122.2M.
> Distance to destination: 1,650.
> ETA: 13.5 days = 28th May.

In my dream, Hugh |Grant was not the Prime Minister from Love Actually (I watched it over about five evenings on Prime downloads). He was a boatbuilder.

Standing in the middle of an enormous factory space, he presented me with an absolutely sparkling 23footer.

In white.

"Well, what colour did you want?" he said.

I don't think we had discussed a colour. Come to that, had I ordered a new boat at all?

"It's the Americans, you see," he went on. "They're the only ones who make this new type of fibreglass with this special shine that never fades - and, of course, Americans insist on everything being white. Anyway, it's not for you. It's for your eldest sister."

My sister is 84 and not at all good on her pins (Arthritis - she puts her faith in the doctors and their joint replacement operations rather than my supplement - but we don't argue about it.) Anyway, I don't think she needs a 23footer, no matter how shiny.

Meanwhile, "This is yours." Hugh flung out a hand in the other direction. This time, the most beautiful little mini-cruiser - no more than 19ft, long keel and charcoal grey with a gaff rig, and black sails all set and hanging motionless as if she were at a boat show.

What that was all about, I have no idea. But he did take me below in my sister's shiny white boat. It turned out the interior was for a fully-crewed superyacht: Owner's suite, cabins for ten guests, multiple fridges and freezers for the Cordon-Bleu chef. Stewardesses in mini-culottes…

Clever, these American designers, said Hugh.

* * *

I've been wondering about getting the Aries back to Lean for repair. It's a five-day trip up the Channel and North Sea to Amsterdam - and then I'll be using up my 90-day Shengen allowance while he does the job. What would it cost to send it by courier? I should do that from Ireland - no Brexit paperwork and customs. What if Lean can't repair it? After all, it must have taken a hell of a bang to bend that shaft - and he doesn't make the lift-up version anymore. I don't want the new one - better to change to a Hydrovane… but then I couldn't put the bracket for the Remigo on the centreline. So maybe I should leave that until I know if the Aries can be fixed. Decisions… decisions…

*

The water temperature is 8.7°C, but it's still only 10° in the cabin. However, I must be getting used to it - last night it was distinctly hot and clammy, fully clothed in the serious sleeping bag. At four o'clock, I had to get up and take off the trousers and sweater (which still left three layers).

I'll tell you who doesn't like it - those little black bugs. The two bags of rice and the couscous are still unopened and stowed in isolation in the tins locker, but now I look closely, I see the bugs have stopped crawling around helping themselves.

They are still there - hundreds of them. But now they're not moving.

Well, they wouldn't be, wouldn't they? The standard advice for a tropical cockroach infestation is: "Go and cruise the Baltic."

I've frozen them to death.

Unfortunately, the cold has had the same effect on the bean sprouts. I managed to get one batch started - and then thought I'd better eat them while I had the chance. But this new batch has swollen, started to split open - and then gone into hibernation. Now they are beginning to smell.

But we are making excellent progress. With a following wind, one reef in each sail and the headsail goose-winged, it's going to be another 120-mile day.

And I seem to be back in civilisation - two ships in two days!

Day 30

> Thursday 15th May 2025.
> 46°46.552'N 40°54.636'W.
> Wind W5. Barometer: 1010.
> Day's Run: 150M.
> Total: 3,694M.
> Average: 123.1M.
> Distance to Destination: 1,501M.
> ETA: 12.2 days = 27th May.

It's all very well having satellite communications, but it does give you a lot of information - and with information comes the need for decisions.

Today is Thursday. On Saturday, a gale is forecast - right where I'm going to be at 1200hrs on Saturday.

Naturally, I adjusted the course - 10° to Starboard in the hope of passing below it. However, the only sure way of avoiding it is to slow right down - at the moment I'm doing 150 miles a day. If I dropped down to 50, it would pass ahead of me on its way to Greenland.

But that would add two days to the voyage - two missed days of lunatics on motorcycles. I would miss Mad Sunday.

This is not an exact science: For one thing, a lot can happen, meteorologically speaking, in 48 hours. Also, if there is a way of measuring distances on the Windy app, I don't know about it, so I have to shift to Navionics and measure out the 300 miles I expect to sail at 80°, then compare that to features on the adjacent coastline - in this case, Eggers Cape to Lynaes. Next, in the Windy App, take a tape measure and compare that distance on the screen to the wind-whipped emptiness off the North Atlantic - and hope that it lands in an area of "orange wind", denoting 20-30kts rather than "red wind", which is 30-40kts. What you really want to avoid is the purple stuff (40-50kts).

Purely for the sake of curiosity, it goes on up: White is 50-60kts - and then there's yellow. They don't have anything to represent wind speeds beyond yellow. Beyond yellow, it's sort of academic…

I suppose the sensible thing to do would be to slow down.

I'm sorry, but I just don't do slowing down. I suppose it could be said that I don't do sensible either. Sensible is boring - and I certainly don't do boring.

So, at the moment, we are off course by 10°, and if things still look the same tomorrow, I shall root out the SeaBrake from under the storm sails in the focsle.

The good thing about it all is that the wind is going my way, and I don't plan on wasting it. The only imponderable is how Eric is going to cope with a gale - Eric the autopilot, remember?

The problem with a following wind arises when the waves get big enough to push the stern round to leeward and leave the boat broadside on to the waves. That's how you get rolled.

So, first of all, I trail 90metres of warp in a bight, which helps hold the stern up to the wind. When that doesn't work anymore, I let go the end from the windward quarter and instead, launch the SeaBrake drogue. That will slow us right down. Now I can recover the trailing warp and set the SeaBrake from a bridle.

The matter of drogues is a talking point among sailors. In fact, it's every bit as ripe for argument as the choice of anchor. The perceived wisdom is that in "survival storm" conditions, the go-to solution is the Jordan Series Drogue - a long rope with fabric cones sewn along its length. This creates so much drag that it must be anchored to enormous metal plates bolted through the hull (the thickness of the plates and size of the bolts to be calculated as if they were going to suspend the whole weight of the boat - with a safety margin built in.)

The idea is to hold the stern up to the wind no matter how big the wave breaking over the boat.

The whole idea sounds terrifying - there is talk of fitting extra-strong storm boards to the companionway to withstand the force of water breaking over the boat…

I didn't have a Jordan Series Drogue. I had something called a SeaBrake, which operates differently. As the forces on it increase, it cleverly adjusts the amount of resistance it offers. If the boat slows, it opens up to keep the stern to the wind. If an enormous and steep wave arrives (the sort that would crash all over a boat and have her hanging on the end of a series drogue), the SeaBrake will close and allow the boat to pick up speed and outrun the wave - all the while providing enough tension to hold the stern to the wind.

I bought one after reading that John Sanders swore by his. Sanders is the legendary Australian sailor who holds the record for having completed 11 solo circumnavigations (three of them without stopping).

The SeaBrake works very well. I tried it in 33kts on the way from Gran Canaria to La Palma. Of course, 33kts is only red wind…

Finally, I switched off the radar - I've seen three ships in two days. Obviously, they don't think this is iceberg country. Anyway, the water temperature is up to 13°C - not that this has made much difference inside…

*

I was thinking how satisfying it is to be on a boat when everything is going well - everything works as it's supposed to, you don't forget to make up the halyard before sheeting in the mainsail - the headsail furling line has not got itself the wrong side of the preventer.

It was like that at two o'clock in the morning - I don't set an alarm anymore - because with Eric steering a compass course, if the sail trim needs attention, I will wake up to a lot of flapping - or possibly the boat heeling the wrong way and threatening to throw me out or bed.

At two o'clock this morning, it was the flapping. We were carrying full sail in 18kts of apparent wind - and flying downwind at better than six knots, so call that 24 true wind.

I came down again and realised that reefing both sails had taken just ten minutes.

That's the way it's supposed to go.

At four o'clock in the morning, I was woken a second time. This time, I was sleeping in "the coffin". This is a clever arrangement installed by the original owner, the innovative Alfred Maley. Essentially, it is a hinged and padded plank. Either it forms a backrest to the port settee or, if you lie down and swing it over yourself, it is a padded leeboard to stop you falling out of bed.

I liken it to a coffin because it really is no wider than the average person's shoulders. Effectively, you're wedged in there no matter where the boat moves. To get out, you swing it above you, back into its original position - and fall on the floor.

Two minutes later, I was togged up in boots, oilskin trousers and my Musto Snug jacket. Although the decks would be wet, there should be no flying spray, not the way I do things.

First, gybe the main: Let off the preventer, haul in the sheet, put the boat on a new and generous course (but not so generous that she will keep on going round in circles). The boom flicks over. Let it out.

The poled-out headsail takes a bit more work. First, it has to be furled - but with a following wind, it is important not to catch the super zero in it.

These two sails are really too close together, but the engineering involved in a longer bowsprit made it impractical to add any more space between them. I just have to be careful - take it slowly: Let out a few inches of sheet, take in a few inches of furling line…

In particular, do not let the headsail billow out and touch the super zero. If you do this, the big sail will start getting rolled in with the little one until the whole collection jams solid.

Or…

Yes, there is an alternative. I didn't know about it until just after four o'clock this morning, when I switched my gaze (and the beam of the head-torch) from the winch in the cockpit to the furling gear on the bow.

The rotating headsail had picked up just the tiniest pinch of super zero. That tiny pinch was the sacrificial strip - dark blue, lightweight, not structural - a layer of disposable material designed to degrade in the harsh ultra-violet light of the tropics while the sail itself remains undamaged.

After two years in the Caribbean, it was pretty well degraded - with the result that it tore, exposing the high-tech laminate sail within - which now gleefully unfurled the top half of itself into what was now (I took a quick glance at the windspeed indicator) 33kts of apparent wind.

No, things were not going according to plan.

Obviously, the sail had to come off. I went down and unlocked the forehatch - moving anything that might resent getting wet. I let the main right off and put the helm down. The boat doesn't exactly stop when you do this, but it makes life a lot more manageable.

The maximum windspeed advised for flying a super zero is 15kts. So, 33kts was not ideal.

Obviously, the approved method for getting it down is to slacken the halyard just enough for each section of sail as it is gathered and persuaded down the forehatch. If you let the whole thing go, it just ends up in the water to leeward, and - since the boat is now going sideways - under the boat.

I had a spinnaker under the boat once - wrapped round the keel. It was never the same again.

So, I tried really, really hard not to let the super zero go in the water. I had one hand on the halyard with a single turn round the winch, the other hand pulling at the sail, one foot braced against the toe rail - the other foot trying to hold down the next bit of sail.

I think you can probably guess what happened next. The beautiful, expensive Super Zero ended up in the water.

I think it was only because the bottom half was still furled that I got away with it.

Well, I had got away with it so far. But we weren't finished yet. I took a second reef in the main - a second reef in the headsail. The trouble was, the wind was rising faster than I was shortening sail.

I handed the main - flew just a scrap of headsail, but Eric was struggling - grinding this way and that. Without the Aries, it is essential that Eric keeps going. I could help him by trailing the long warp. The question was, how long was this going to go on?

Well, now I've got Starlink, I can find out, can't I? I logged on.

The Windy app had the answer: Basically, 48 hours.

So, it was worth getting out the SeaBrake.

I had given a lot of thought to stowing this. It does fold flat which helps, but I didn't like to scrunch its essential circular shape - so I put it under everything else. Now I don't know where anything is - especially since moving everything that might resent getting wet when I dumped the Super Zero on top of it all. I found it in the end, of course - but only after moving everything all over again, so that now it was all equally wet.

First, I trailed it astern. I've done this before, and it worked very well. This time it didn't. It took a while to establish why: Setting up the bridle involves tying a rolling hitch onto the standing line. Don't use a hard rope to tie a rolling hitch onto a soft rope - it slips.

It was while I was sorting this out, that I began to question the wisdom of running with the wind. According to the Windy map, if I could contrive to stay where I was, the worst of the gale would pass ahead of me.

I should heave-to.

I have never managed to do this successfully. Lyn Pardey swears by it. She and Larry lay hove-to in the most ferocious weather all over the world. They even went down to Cape Horn to prove it worked there. They had their own system of a small parachute anchor on a bridle and a trysail to hold the boat at 45° to the wind while she made a knot-and-a-half of leeway. This caused the long keel to create a slick, which encouraged breaking waves to collapse just as they do on a beach.

I don't have a parachute anchor, but I have read about someone who used a Seaclaw drogue from the bow to hold the boat's head up to the wind and to stop her fore-reaching.

Moving the line from the stern to the bow is something I don't want to talk about (any more than I want to talk about finding the topping lift wrapped round the radar reflector when I went to hoist the trysail). In fact, even *I* don't even want to think about it (other than to remind myself how I'm going to do it next time).

Anyway, for the first time, *Samsara* lay hove to, going gently sideways at one-and-a-half knots and leaving a slick to windward. Of course, she doesn't have as big a slick as the Pardey's *Taleisin* and *Serrafyn* because she doesn't have that "pilot boat" underwater profile and I'm a bit concerned that, even though the wind is now down to about 27kts, I have felt a couple of *bangs* of breaking waves. We shall have to see how I get on in the early hours of tomorrow morning.

Meanwhile, I tidied up the cockpit, put a couple of extra sail ties on the main and went below for breakfast. It was half-past nine, and all this had started at four o'clock in the morning.

Come to think of it, I've been sailing all day, every day for a month. I deserve a day off.

Day 31

> Friday 16th May 2025.
> 47°45.421'N 38°25.428'W.
> Wind: NW7. Barometer: 1017.
> Day's Run: 117M.
> Total: 3,811M.
> Average: 122.9M.
> Distance to Destination: 1,384.
> ETA: 11.3 days = 27th May.

For the first time, that log entry was not made at noon. But I don't think it makes much difference - I haven't been going anywhere. At ten o'clock in the morning, I went back to bed - peeled off the trousers with the wet knees (why is it that all oilskins leak at the knees). I did keep the long johns with the wet knees, reasoning that they would dry in the sleeping bag - which they did. I once heard that soldiers sleep with their boots in the bottom of their sleeping bags, so they're not frozen when they have to put them on in the morning.

The alarm went off just before twelve, but today is a day off, so I just lay there, marvelling at this restful new motion. There's a bit of rocking, but the overwhelming sensation is one of the boat just bobbing on the waves - as placid as a seabird taking a rest.

All through the late afternoon and evening, the wind increased. Dinner was a bit of a trial - the motion being every bit as bad as if we were sailing. I opened my one tin of peaches -

judging this to be a special occasion. I was in bed by ten o'clock. Once again, I didn't set an alarm - if I needed to get up, I should know all about it.

The gale struck in the small hours of the morning. I know that because that's when the windy app said it would. I didn't look at my watch because getting your wrist up by your face in a sleeping bag when you've only got the width of your shoulders to do it in is just nothing but unnecessary effort. In fact, I didn't get out of bed until eight o'clock the next morning - a full ten hours. I think it might be a record - and then only because the wind charger was switching itself on and off all the time because the batteries were full, and it needed to dump electricity.

If that was the greatest of my problems, then I really didn't have much to worry about. I opened the hatch - which took a bit of doing because of the boom lying on it - and was greeted by a classical wind-swept seascape. It was not as dramatic as the "worst summer storm" off the Hebrides in 2000, but it was still pretty impressive: Bright sunshine, breaking waves as far as the eye could see - and, now I looked at the wind instrument - 38kts.

The boat was lying at 60° to the wind, which is still a bit too much broadside - 45° would be better, but I didn't see what I could do about it. The tiller was lashed as far to leeward as it would go. The trysail was sheeted hard in, and no headsail - so all the effort was aft of the mast. And then there was the SeaBrake set from a point as far forward as I could manage - what else was I supposed to do?

Of course, a drogue offers only a fraction of the resistance of a parachute anchor, so maybe that's where my plan is flawed - although it worked in the account of the Sea Claw.

Certainly, I didn't have the "dry decks" described by Lin Pardey.

I was thinking about all this and telling myself that at least I hadn't been hit by a big breaking crest - when I was hit by a big breaking crest. There was a *bang*. Things flew from one side to the other, and I was pitched from my seat on the windward berth.

I would like it recorded that I had the presence of mind to twist in mid-flight like a cat getting ready to land on its feet - although in my case, the priority was to position my back to the woodwork on the other side rather than trying to save myself with my hands and break a wrist.

Interestingly, while writing that, I had the opportunity to witness two more waves coming aboard. I could see them through the skylight, and they came at an acute angle - no worse than sailing into a rough sea - *Samsara's* big bow punching most of the power out of them. Having looked at the plotter earlier and seen how we have changed course through about 60° since all this started, I think the problem arises when the boat is lying at 60° to the wind, but the swell is still coming from more like 90°. It's bound to happen when the wind veers - and by implication, I would have been better on starboard tack when the wind shift would have reduced the wave angle, not increased it.

Now that I have weather forecasts, I can use this: I can choose which tack to set the trysail based on whether the wind is due to veer or back.

Meanwhile, they say it's going to moderate by midday, and then I'll get another forecast and decide whether to sit tight for another 24 hours or get going again.

I'm not complaining. The worst I've had to put up with is a bit of flapping sprayhood that needed to be tucked in and the occasional drip from the centre hatch, which always seems to land in the most inconvenient place. Right now, I seem to be catching most of it on a kapok cushion - I'll just have to remember not to sit on it.

Day 32

> Saturday 17th May 2025.
> 48°02.581'N 38°09.938'W,
> Wind: NW7. Barometer: 1004.
> Day's Run: 20M.
> Total: 3,831M.
> Average: 119.7M
> Distance to Destination: 1,366M.
> ETA: 11.4 days = 29th May.

Well, it's over. The highest windspeed I saw was 38kts first thing this morning, and after that it moderated steadily - down to less than 30kts by the midday log entry. But, oh my, what a sea it's left. I really don't fancy going up to the foredeck to recover the SeaBrake.

The midday forecast still offers "orange wind", and the trouble with that is that it's not enough of a change to let the sea go down - and unless it does, I can't see Eric coping very well. The Aries would be fine. That reacts instantly - you can see a twitch on the vane translated immediately to the pulling of the tiller line. Eric has to process everything through his microchips and circuit boards. These big waves aren't going to wait for that.

The Windy forecast suggested the quickest way out of this was to go south - but first I would have to get sailing again.

I waited until two o'clock before kitting myself up in my (only partially dry) trousers, oilskins and all. I think I was an hour too early on the foredeck. For one thing, it was going up and down by a good two metres every two or three seconds, and every time it went down, it seemed to scoop up a bucket of water.

I'm going to reorganise the lines for the drogue. The present system is far too complicated. The whole process took an hour, but I reckon I can get it down to half that (I'm told that recovering a Jordan Series Drogue can take two). It was fascinating to watch it once I had winched it close to the boat: When the strain came on it (and I couldn't make any progress even with the winch in low gear), I could see the way it collapsed, reducing the drag and allowing the boat to speed up.

Of course, the biggest surprise after all that effort is how easy it is to bring it aboard backwards by hooking the loop of the floating line attached to the crown.

So that left us hove-to under trysail - but now at more than 90° to the wind, so that the bigger waves crashed right into the cockpit.

I went below for a cup of tea and chipped off a lump of Nutella before setting about handing the trysail - much less trouble (until it comes to taking it below and flaking it back into its bag. For a small sail, it does take up a lot of room.)

By this time, *Samsara* had assumed her default position relative to the wind - bow down, wind on the quarter. My plan for going southeast to get out of the blow called for a course pretty much dead downwind. First, I tried a scrap of headsail on the basis that the boat ought to "weathercock" and find her own way.

That didn't work. Nor did steering further to the south to stop her gybing - we just ended up going further and further up into the wind while Eric put on a good show of grinding and groaning, but without really making any difference. Maybe the problem was that we just weren't going fast enough - there wasn't enough water flowing over the rudder. I gave her some more sail, and that seemed to improve things. I went below for another cup of tea - this one with a slug of rum in it.

Even the rum failed to cheer me up. Partly, because the plotter showed the "distance to destination" was not decreasing - we were going at right angles to where we wanted to go. This was because I had decided I wanted to go southeast to get out of the orange wind. What if the orange wind wasn't going to be where I thought it was?

What I needed was another forecast - even though it was only four hours since the last one. Every time I log onto Windy, it costs me in data payments to Mr Musk. This I resent hugely. However, today I discovered that most of the bills come from downloading videos of Lottie's wild social life in Hanoi.

She is over there, teaching English to little children - and having a wonderful a time according to the videos she to uploads to the family WhatsApp group. Since I am paying for data by the gigabyte, I don't open them. But then, this afternoon, I clicked on one when I was not online, and it played! They had been downloading in the background, so I must have paid for them anyway!

On this basis, downloading a weather forecast - a forecast, I might add, rather more important than a bunch of twenty-somethings toasting each other in silly cocktails.

The new forecast did indeed show I was heading for more orange wind (as well as not making any progress). I might just as well make the most of the orange wind, and go where I want to go…

Eric seems to be coping with it - certainly there's plenty of water flowing over the rudder: We're doing a steady six knots.

I just wish I hadn't stood there for so long, marvelling at the readout on the plotter over the chart table, instead of slotting in the washboard and shutting the hatch and putting the kettle on for yet another cup of tea.

Because, just at that moment, another enormous wave crashed into the cockpit and poured straight in, all over the chart table. It missed me by inches, but the log book will never be the same again.

*

After the storm has passed, there is supposed to be a period of calm - a hot meal, the cook cleans up the galley. Clothes hang around the cabin to dry. It is a time for relaxing - maybe a tot to celebrate coming through unscathed.

But the storm didn't let go - not completely. Like a losing player who keeps on grousing long after the final whistle, the wind would appear to settle at 18kts - and then suddenly puff up to 30 (but only for long enough for me to climb into soggy oilies and present myself for duty in the cockpit. Then it would meekly return to "moderate westerly".

This happened again and again. I began to mutter.

The worst part was that these occasional bouts of Force 7 would not allow the sea state to moderate as it should. Enormous waves still roared past like express trains. I swear one of them was twice as high as my head as I stood in the cockpit hanging onto the mainsheet as if I was on a fairground ride.

The one bright spot was that Eric was proving to be a much better helmsman than I had given him credit for. I mentioned earlier that he cannot react as fast as the Aries because he has to "think" (yes, that is the right word - after all, human thought is no more than a series of electrical impulses. It's just that Eric's run on 12volts).

It is now clear that he has the measure of these waves and, rather than try and react fast enough to counter them, he simply waits, knowing that as they pass under the boat, they will first push the stern off course, and then the bow - and leave the boat pointing in the same direction as before. Only then does he tweak the course if necessary.

If he can keep this up all the way, I will write to Raymarine and give him a good report.

But helping in the galley is not within his job description. I have never known an evening like it. In the end, the place was such a mess that I gave up and left the spilt peppers down the side of the engine casing, congealing kidney beans glueing the washing up liquid bottle to the olive oil - and over in the still-wet navstation, mashed potato all over the hand-bearing compass.

I couldn't face clearing up. I'd probably just make more mess - that's the sort of thing that happens when a washing-up bowl takes flight.

I didn't even clean my teeth - just peeled off the damp outer layer and climbed into the big sleeping bay, pulled over the plank to shut myself in the coffin - and pretended I was somewhere else.

Then the heads door started banging.

You can't ignore something like that - even when it's not just a matter of slipping out of bed, padding across the carpet and closing it. When, instead, you have to haul the plank back over so you can get your feet over the edge of the bunk and then reach for the pole at the edge of the chart table because you can't stand unaided. After that, you have to step straight out of the sleeping bag into your Crocs because the floor is wet and, so far, your socks are dry.

Then fasten the head door and repeat steps one to ten or whatever it is, in reverse.

If I did this once, I must have done it half a dozen times during the course of the night. I tried wedging the door with a dismantled clothes peg, a wad of paper…

I did not use the loop of shock cord and the little hook that some previous owner had installed for just this purpose. I could have done. I should have done, but would you believe, I forgot all about it.

So, what with all these disturbances, it was a disjointed sort of night. Maybe that explains the episodic nature of the dream - and the fact that the episodes weren't in the right order.

It was back with the newspaper theme. Heaven knows why. I haven't worked in a newspaper office for thirty years. Anyway, this office wasn't an office at all but some sort of cavernous warehouse - all dark and dusty with corrugated iron walls and the editor's office up in the eaves at the top of a lot of metal stairs.

The editor was a woman with long hair sprayed to the consistency of titanium and horn-rimmed glasses. She kept tapping her chin with her pen (I don't know her name, but I last saw her playing the interviewer in a film called *She's Funny That Way* that I downloaded on Prime). She called down to me and said to get over to the USS Nimitz, which was anchored in Falmouth Bay while President Trump visited the town: Take a photographer and get over there now.

"I can't," I said.

Why not

"Because I've got my hands handcuffed behind my back."

They were, too - with a chain. I could bring my hands to my sides, but not much further. I certainly was in no fit state to go and interview Trump. Can you imagine what he'd have to say? He's probably ship me off to El Salvador without even taking off the handcuffs.

The editor wanted to know who had handcuffed me - she shouted down from the top of the stairs. I was standing on the floor of the warehouse, looking like an idiot and, now I see, wearing some sort of grey prison fatigues.

Worse than that, I couldn't even say who had handcuffed me: "One of the snappers, for a prank…"

The nameless photographers all chorused that it had been Dan Maskell (wasn't he a tennis commentator?) Anyway, the luckless Dan was shamed into releasing me, and together we got into a RIB moored just outside the warehouse/office - and set off for the Nimitz.

You may be interested to know that the Nimitz apparently looks like a saucepan but many, many stories high - in fact so high that, from sea level you can only just see the tail of an aeroplane on the flight deck.

I wound up the big outboard, and soon we were bouncing over the waves to the boarding ladder on the other side.

This seemed to take a long time. The Nimitz was indeed so huge that I thought I was closer than I was. Apparently, I thought I was practically there and in fact I was still five miles away and about to run out of fuel - but I can't think about that now. The heads' door is banging…

There is another episode in which this frightening editor says: "Bang out a quick piece for the first edition before you go."

It now appears that this is not the Falmouth Packet - the legendary local paper that still serves that part of remote Cornwall, but some typical small-town American paper as thrown onto front porches all over the States by kids on bicycles.

I wrote: "It is with great pride that the (insert name of newspaper) has been chosen to break the news that the President of the United States is visiting the giant aircraft carrier USS Nimitz…"

- He's been here all day, hasn't he? said the editor.

"Yes, but there's been a news blackout. We're the first to report it."

- No, we're not. It's been all over the BBC. This is no damn good. What are you playing at?"

I believe I crawled back under a stone. I never did get to see Mr Trump - not even his hair.

Day 33

Sunday 18th May 2025.
48°33.769'N. 35°50.965'W.
Wind: SW4. Barometer: 1004.
Day's Run: 98M.
Total 3,929M.
Average: 119.1M.
Distance to Destination: 1,272M.
ETA: 10.7 days = 28th May.

Isn't it strange what pleases some people? This afternoon, I spent two-and-a-half hours on deck. To begin with, it was raining and I started off by recovering the SeaBrake - which, I'm pleased to say, I did all by hand, with no help at all from the cockpit winch.

Once that was below, I unfurled some more headsail. Eric was doing so well, he could cope - but then the wind dropped again, so I rolled it all up and hoisted the main once more. First, I hoisted it with the two reefs that were still tied down from last time, unrolled the headsail, then decided I'd done it all on the wrong tack, so gybed, changed the pole over and re-set the headsail and preventer on the other side.

Then I thought the starboard preventer/downhaul was seriously chafed where it had spent too long rubbing itself against the shroud while I slept on, oblivious to a middle-of-the-night gybe.

So, I swapped it for the super zero sheet, which I won't be using until the sail gets repaired.

Then I decided the main didn't need two reefs, so I took out the second.

While all this was going on, the topping lift was still niggling away at the back of my mind. You may remember, it was hooked around the radar reflector, which means I can't use it as an emergency main halyard... and part of the reason I still had one reef was because I wanted to spare the chafed part of the halyard where it passes over the sheave when the sail is fully hoisted.

I really, really don't want to go up the mast, but a moderate following wind would surely blow it free if I gave it enough slack and a bit of jiggling.

OK, so it took a lot of slack and ten minutes of jiggling, and what I had not realised was that the (now lazy) super zero halyard wasn't helping. But I got it all done and (for extra stones in the pot), locking the shackle again with cable ties.

As you can imagine, all of this involved a good deal of scampering around the deck, standing up at the mast, using both hands and having to find some other way of holding on because, 750 miles south of Greenland, less than 24 hours after a full gale, there were still some pretty big waves around and when one of those passed under the boat, oh my: Over we would go - 25°...35°...

It is at times like these that you start thinking about what happens if you do fall over. The boat is making six knots. I know I can't catch a boat doing even two knots - not if she's got a head start on me, even if the water is now up to 12.6°C - not if I've got to climb back aboard at the end of it.

So, then you start thinking about watching the boat sailing on her way - from a viewpoint 20cm above the water. Of course, you would only be able to see her from the top of a wave. It wouldn't take long before even the top of the mast disappeared.

That sort of thing doesn't half make you hold on.

While we're on the subject of tangled halyards, do you know why so many halyards get tangled at the top of the mast? It is because the foredeck crew have trained themselves not to look up because their baseball hats will blow off. I really must publish this as an addendum to Passmore's Law of Lost Hats.

You can find The Law in my seminal work, *Old Man Sailing*, available from all good online bookstores - and with any luck, at a discount on the "Bookshop" page of my blog once I get it set up.

Oddly enough, writing that has pushed me into rooting through the pile of clothes and cushions jammed behind the charcoal heater: Did I really lose my *Babiana* hat (given me by my cousin, the cook on the superyacht). I can see it clearly in my mind's eye, sinking astern - surprisingly quickly - and then there is the urge to dive over the side after it…

Equally clearly, I remember using this as the theme for a little lecture to the crew, which included my grandson, who is about to take his Competent Crew course - although, what they were doing on what is supposed to be a singlehanded voyage, I couldn't quite work out.

It was a dream, of course. The *Babiana* cap is still here, safe and sound (I know better than to wear it for halyard jiggling).

Sorry, but the following morning, the topping lift was back round the radar reflector. It seems the "anti-snarl-up" line, which stretches down the front of the reflector and back to the mast above and below, has given way. I could solve the problem by making sure I kept the topping lift tight at all times. It's an option. First, I find myself in the odd position of actually hoping for a calm so that I'll be forced to drop the main - and while it's down I'll end-for-end the halyard.

*

At last - the evening beer in the cockpit - with ten knots of following wind, brilliant sunshine and the sprayhood folded flat. The only disappointment was having to wear four layers of clothing and a woolly hat. But it does show that life on board is improving.

Also, I was able to finish my book without constantly watching the waves, wondering which one was going to soak me.

The book, incidentally - Daphne du Maurier's *Rebecca* - I finished at a rush, desperate to know what happened next. It must be so sad to be an intellectual and to have read all the good stuff before you finished university. I was on such a high that I even read the fiercely scholastic *Afterword* - it's one way of coming down to earth.

Day 34

>Monday 19th May 2025.
>45°05.252'N 33°18.702'W.
>Wind W3. Barometer: 1012.
>Day's Run: 107M.
>Total: 4,036M.
>Average: 118.7M.
>Distance to Destination: 1,168M.
>ETA: 9.8 days = 29th May.

Less than ten days to go, and I'm definitely not going to run out of beer. I had to unscrew the cabin sole today because there was none to hand, which means I must have got through about 70 cans. The time had come to broach the bottles (I seem to remember there were about 30 down there) - and what do I find? Two more six-packs of Balboa!

I added a dozen bottles of Heineken to the ready-use locker while I was at it - I can't see myself wanting to unscrew the floor again in the first flush of arriving.

According to my calculations, the spaghetti, noodles and instant mashed potato should see me out as well, so I should be able to throw the two packets of rice and one of couscous with the (dead) bugs into the marina skip.

Another surprise: I just took off a layer because I was too hot. That hasn't happened in what seems like living memory.

A glance at the cabin thermometer: Amazing! It's 16°C!

*

It's half-past nine and I've only just finished breakfast - but then, I only got up at 9.30… having gone to bed at 9.30 p.m.

Yes, that is a full twelve hours. It was so bloody cold, I didn't want to get up. I had nowhere to be and nothing in particular that I had to do, considering the wind had remained pretty constant on a broad reach all night.

I did have to get up at two o'clock when I awoke as we gybed - and it did seem there was a lot more flapping than usual. Sliding the hatch back for a quick peek at the wind instrument: it was blowing 30kts.

It had done this two or three times during the day as wind squalls blew through (which was why I was so well-practised at getting into oilies). Even so, by the time I got out there, it was raining hard and, by the time, I had a reef in, the wind was beginning to ease - *if the wind before the rain, soon you may make sail again…*

I left the reef - it was still blowing 15kts apparent.

But apart from that, I spent a very peaceful night - more so than the one before, when I had a 70ml bottle of honey in bed with me.

No, I am not going to describe some little-known sexual practice. The problem is that it is so damn cold, runny honey won't run, and in Panama they sell it in wine-bottle sizes. I need it in a little plastic squeezy container that will fit in the galley rack. The only solution is to decant it - and the only way to do that at 10°C is to sleep with it.

But last night, as I say, was a marathon. I went to bed at 2130 because I was watching *When Harry Met Sally* on my phone (because the iPad has "detected moisture" in its charging port). Given that the thing can connect with Lottie in Vietnam from the middle of the Atlantic, you'd think someone would possess the know-how to keep the water out.

Anyway, I've seen *When Harry Met Sally* so many times that when it came to the "orgasm in the diner" scene, I really couldn't be bothered (and thought it would be a nice start to the next episode). By the way, did you know the woman who says: "I'll have what she's having", was the director Rob Reiner's mother - he couldn't imagine anyone saying it better.

I mention this because today marks the 35th day I have not spoken to another living soul, and it is interesting to note how introspective this has made me. For instance, recalling that fact about my favourite film (yes, it would be the one for the Desert Island), I remember when I said the same thing in a restaurant: The Evening Standard had been given a tip that Margaret Thatcher had booked a table at the Ritz. I was to go "just to observe," as the news editor put it. "Imagine if something happened and we'd wasted the tip."

I took the books editor as cover, and we had a good view of Mrs T, her son Mark and their guest seated at a table on a slightly higher level than the "ordinary" diners - as places like The Ritz like to do with their more celebrated customers.

Remarking to the waiter that "I see Mrs Thatcher is here tonight," and hoping that he was a gossipy sort of waiter (he wasn't), I asked what they had ordered.

"I'm sorry sir, but all our guests' orders are confidential."

This was no good at all. What on earth was I supposed to write about - even if I was only there to "observe".

So, I said: "I'll have what she's having."

Dover sole and a bottle of Montrachet.

Why I am telling you this, I have no idea - put it down to isolation syndrome. At least I am stopping short of launching into last night's many dreams - there was, after all, plenty of time for them. But they were all newspaper dreams and this is supposed to be a sailing book not *Tedious Reminiscences of a Boring Old Hack*.

I thought for a moment in the cockpit that we had some real excitement. I had just reefed and settled *Samsara* back on her course and stood there, holding onto the two handles mounted at the back end of the coachroof, when I began thinking how extraordinarily well Eric was handling his very important job.

Look at him - just sitting there, ignoring the small course corrections, saving his amps for the important stuff.

Actually, now I came to think about it, I hadn't heard a peep out of him for five minutes. This might not be surprising because the wind seemed to have dropped - the boat nodding along on her placid way. It was quite some time before I looked at the compass and realised we were way off course.

Oh no! (I actually said "Oh no!" out loud). My greatest fear had been realised. Eric had packed up, so I was going to have to hand-steer for a thousand miles—or open the *Singlehanded Tips* book saved on my Kindle for just this eventuality. It has whole chapters on how to boom out the storm jib to windward and connect it to the tiller with counter-balancing bungees.

Or I could make a proper effort at repairing the Aries - I would have the time, after all. I would certainly have the incentive.

Instead, I checked to see that Eric was on duty and found "Standby" on his screen.

I switched him on, and off we went again.

I think I might dedicate this book to Eric - if he gets us there…

Now it is eleven o'clock and time for coffee - except there isn't any.

Well, there is. Of course there is. I have two kilos of finest Colombian coffee beans.

The trouble is that I have a rechargeable coffee grinder that won't charge. This has nothing to do with moisture in the charging port. It's just broken.

Infuriatingly, it's only a couple of months old - ordered from Amazon after I couldn't find one anywhere in Santa Marta. Getting a rechargeable one was a bit ridiculous anyway, but I hadn't had the Lithium batteries for long and was only just beginning to realise the full range of the electrical possibilities which they open up. I could just buy an ordinary one and plug it in - but I'd been trying to get a rechargable one since Trinidad (before Lithium). I suppose I just got fixated.

Anyway, it doesn't help me now. I don't even have a pestle and mortar. Can you smash coffee beans with a hammer on the chopping board - or would the pieces just fly all over the cabin creating a sensation I remember from when the children were young: walking on Lego in bare feet.

Meanwhile, I am down to the last three redbush teabags. After that, it's on to the emergency supply of Puerto Lindo's Chinese Black Tea.

Day 35

> Tuesday 20th May 2025.
> 50°02.573'N 30°38.328'W.
> Wind: SE2. Barometer: 1016.
> Day's Run: 119M.
> Total: 4,155.
> Average: 118.7M.
> Distance to Destination: 1,050.
> ETA: 8.8 days = 29th May.

Not so good: At about mid-afternoon, close-hauled with 18-20kts apparent, the boat kept putting herself about. This happens sometimes - even when Eric is set to follow the wind rather than the compass, but now I seemed to be out there every ten minutes.

I decided the "wind mode" wasn't working - sometimes the screen announces "No navigation data". But even though I gave him a generous allowance on the compass course (for Iceland), he still kept putting us about.

It wasn't until mid-afternoon that it dawned on me, the Eric wasn't working.

Or to put it at its bleakest: I had 890 miles to go and no self-steering.

Obviously, the first thing to do was give the boat a try - maybe *Samsara* would steer herself. Certainly, she can keep going for a remarkable length of time when the Aries chain slips off, or the whole clamp drops off the tiller because it's intended for a much bigger boat.

So, I eased the traveller down its track a bit and let the tiller swing.

She's doing really very well - with a certain amount of flapping and shaking, we're doing four knots for the Faeroes. At least it meant I could stop listening to Spanish lessons and think about what to do.

Obviously, I can't steer for that long and negotiating the North Channel into the Irish Sea is not recommended for people who can't keep their eyes open. I could make for Galway - anchor at Inishmore for a kip before a day sail up Galway Bay.

The SeaBrake is supposed to have an emergency steering function - you haul on one side of the bridle or the other. I tried it. You need the lines on winches, and I don't have enough of them. I did think I might put them through the spare headsail fairleads and back to the halyard winches by the companionway. Surely that would be better for steering anyway - having the pivot point in the middle. But I haven't tried it.

Before I do, I ought to have another look at the Aries. Thinking about it since giving up and consigning its bits to the focsle, I really can't understand why it wouldn't work. The shaft still turns even if it is bent - so why should it turn more one way than the other? And anyway, does that matter? So, it might not work as well as it should when trying to turn in one direction, but it's got to be better than nothing.

I thought about getting the main frame inboard again - or bolting the paddle back on in situ… or just turning it upside down for another look. None of these options appealed with 20kts across the deck and the sea getting up to match.

I could give Eric a rest.

I took his steering arm off and brought it below, wiped it lovingly with a tea towel and put him to bed in the locker by the navigator's seat. Then I realised that I was only resting his steering arm. His control unit, his electronic compass - they were still hard at work. That's when it occurred to me that I didn't know how to turn him off. Normally, he goes off when I press the "instruments" button. I examined the screen and the buttons below. One appeared to be a "power" symbol.

Of course, I could get the instructions out.

Or I could be lazy and hope that if I plugged everything back in and switched on, everything would be all right again.

Besides, the flapping and banging of *Samsara* steering herself is driving me mad.

Well, I got out Eric's instruction manual and turned to page 98: *Troubleshooting*. As you can imagine, there was a lot about good connections and the latest software. I did find something about "Factory Reset" and so I navigated the menu on the display and pressed "Select". Everything went quiet for a bit, and then came back to the way it was before. To show willing, I tacked and then gybed us round in a circle to help the compass orient itself, but to no avail. The compass readout on the display bears no resemblance to the ship's compass. I don't think we can count on Eric any longer - not as an enthusiastic helmsman. He's certainly not going to get a book dedicated to him.

So instead, I upended the Aries and inspected it all over again. There's no doubt that the shaft won't turn the paddle to starboard, and I have no idea why. I will email Lean in Amsterdam to see if he has any advice, but I think we can write that off as well.

Meanwhile, I have used the chain to peg the tiller slightly to windward and we're doing really quite well in 22kts - as good a course as I could expect - and making four-and-a-half knots. I've had another look at the forecast and, apparently, I can expect moderate following winds tomorrow afternoon when I will give Eric another try. I did have a brief look at the Raymarine website, but I don't think it would be much more help than the manual.

It would be nice to talk to a technician, but you can imagine how long I would have to wait and listen to music - and how many of Mr Musk's gigabytes that would cost.

I might write to Dave Jones, though. He installed the thing. He might have some ideas.

Meanwhile, somebody did once say that Passmore would do anything for good copy…

Then I went out into the cockpit to see if there was some other way of going in the right direction - however slowly. That was when I spied what I took to be an extremely small flying fish in the scupper drain. It didn't occur to me that we are far too far north for flying fish - that's just the sort of fish I'm used to seeing lying around on deck. Although I did find a tiny squid earlier today.

But guess what? It wasn't a fish. It was a machine screw.

Finding screws and bolts and clevis pins - and any other kind of fastening on deck is always a worry. Usually, I have no idea where they came from - which is doubly worrying.

But this one I recognised instantly. I became very familiar with the type after the knockdown north of the Canaries (see The Voyage #2). It was one of the two screws that fastens the boom to the gooseneck. So, it's kind of important.

My first thought was: What a piece of luck. It hadn't fallen over the side. Obviously, it had shaken itself out with all the mainsail flapping that had been going on. The question was, how to put it back with the wind blowing 22kts, the boat rolling all over the place - and, of course, no self-steering.

I could write about how not to do it, but it would take too long (it took me an hour researching that topic).

So here is how to replace a machine screw in a gooseneck 988 miles west of Land's End.

Take a line from the end of the boom through a spinnaker block and onto a winch. Pull the boom back until the holes match horizontally (this will take half a dozen trips back and forth).

Pass a line under the front of the boom, up through the spinnaker pole ring and down to the winch on the mast. Crank up the boom until the holes are aligned vertically.

Now go back to the cockpit winch because the vertical alignment has mucked up the horizontal alignment… and then back and forth to the mast. Carry on doing this for a bit.

Then, just pop the screw in.

Don't be daft. It's not going to be that easy.

But, trust me; the thread will engage - and then, with the big screwdriver (with the hexagonal shaft) and the 8mm spanner, the whole edifice is forced into alignment.

I should add that I couldn't get it all the way home - that would be too perfect - but I will be inspecting it daily.

Finally, as darkness fell, it was a matter of getting the boat settled and going in the right direction for the night. The wind had gone round to the south, and I wanted to steer 072°. After a bit of experimenting and delaying not only the evening beer but also dinner, I now have us on the way to Ireland at an average speed of 1.6 knots under just a double-reefed headsail and with the tiller on the chain four links to weather.

It'll do for now.

Dinner was rather a sombre affair - the last carrot. Was it such a good idea to throw away that opened bag of rice (and its bugs)? After all, how long is this going to take? Think about it: 1,050 miles at 1.6kts? That's 27 days. When it came to preparing tomorrow's breakfast, I measured out three spoonfuls of oats instead of four. Two spoonfuls of peanuts instead of three. How long can I eke out the Nutella? It's not great lumps I crave - just a taste of chocolate…

And so, I slept soundly from 0030 to 0630 - there was no point in alarms. I knew we were going to be off course (by about 50°). At least we weren't going backwards.

Meanwhile, I opened the Kindle to see if the book on emergency self-steering was still there. I downloaded it years ago, thinking I might need it one day.

The book is called, somewhat laboriously, *Thoughts, Tips, Techniques & Tactics for Singlehanded Sailing* by Andrew Evans (Third Edition). It was not published with Kindle software, so the whole page, as it appears in the printed edition, is reduced to the size of a Kindle screen. This means it is like reading the ingredients on an American bottle of fizzy drink. I got out the magnifying glass.

Sure enough, there seemed to be a fairly simple system involving the storm jib set off the windward bow cleat with the sheet going through a series of blocks to the tiller.

But in daylight, I planned to make a final effort with Eric. Now that the sea was quieter, I would swing his electronic compass by motoring in a circle three times, "each circle taking three minutes to complete", according to the book. I furled the headsail, switched him on, navigated his menu, started the engine - and discovered there was no water coming out of the exhaust. Sure enough, in the time it had taken to do that, the water temperature had gone up from 11.8°C in the sea to 34°C in the exhaust pipe. I switched off.

There was water coming out of the impeller - which, to my not very mechanical mind, suggested two solutions.

    1. Replace the thermostat (I have a spare, but will have to find out where it goes).

    2. Treat the engine with muriatic acid. This was on the list before leaving Panama - necessary but not urgent.

Obviously, it makes sense to try the acid first (it needs doing anyway), but that is something that should definitely not be tried at sea - even in an anchorage, if there is a chance of anyone driving past in a RIB at 16kts. The stuff is designed to dissolve "organic material" like barnacles and…er…people.

So, if it's still overheating, I shall have to stop outside the harbour and ask for a tow.

Of course, if I had some way of attaching the Remigo to the stern, the problem wouldn't arise…

I put the engine casing back together, collected the screwdrivers and whatnot and looked out into the cockpit to see the tiller at dead centre and Eric twitching it quietly this way and that. I looked at the plotter "GPS Heading 073°"

With an east-going current, that would be about right. In other words, Eric is working again. I sat and watched him. I unfurled the rest of the headsail. The speed jumped to three-and-a-half knots. The course remained constant.

I felt a little foolish about the email I had sent to Dave Jones. In a rush of enthusiasm, I was about to hoist the main, but something like this would surely have emptied the pot. It was time for another stone.

By the way, if this business of "Stones in the Pot" is all a mystery to you, there's a blog post all about it.

Instead of hoisting the main, I recovered the halyard by using the staysail halyard as a messenger - I'll have to go up the mast and put it back when I get in, but that's easy. It's not internal.

Now the main halyard is back. I didn't end-for-end it in the end (what a great sentence!) The chafed patch was so close to the splice that it wouldn't have saved much. But I did have to measure out new reefing markers and sew them on (so, there's another stone!) The shackle is tied with a proper halyard knot. I had to look it up, and learned that it is "very hard to undo" - well, so is a splice. I'll cut it off if I ever need to.

Something else I discovered while I was doing the "tour of inspection" (yet another stone): Twenty-four hours hove-to, hanging on the end of the SeaBrake managed to bend the screws in the bow fairlead and cracked the teak toe rail. Obviously, there is a fair bit of weight on it even though it is designed to "give". Maybe the "weight" comes before the "give". Anyway, next time, the line will have to go straight to the cleat, and I'll need a length of split plastic hose to clip over the rail. Don't you just love the learning curve?

Day 36

> Wednesday 21st May 2025.
> 50°27.115'N 27°11.493'W.
> Wind SW6. Barometer 1018.
> Day's Run: 60M.
> Total: 4,215M.
> Average: 117.1M.
> Distance to Destination: 990M.
> ETA: 8 days = 29th May.

How things can change in 24 hours! Six+ knots on course for Inchtrahull with 26kts of wind behind us over an essentially calm sea - absolutely flying with Eric steering immaculately. I think he was offended that I doubted him and now wants to get back in the skipper's good books.

This morning's comms session brought an email from Dave Jones - it seems that, rummaging around in the sailmaker's locker, I may have moved something metallic so that it was right next to the electronic compass on the other side of the bulkhead - then I was in there again this morning, so maybe I moved it back. It makes sense.

Also, Lean in Amsterdam says that Mark Slats, who so nearly won the first Golden Globe race with an Aries, overcame a similar problem by over-compensating with the steering angle. Anyway, he seems to think he can fix it.

So, now I can celebrate with two beers. I might even treat myself to half an onion instead of a quarter tonight!

One other thing: I won't have to wait so long - we're up to 30°W already, and the clocks go forward another hour. It really is amazing how much faster you cover the ground up here in the north compared to a trade wind crossing.

*

Well, that was quite a night! Possibly because I had been to bed so late the previous night (after a day fraught with Eric's problems and the gooseneck), I turned in at half-past nine. I had been watching the last of *When Harry Met Sally,* and the trouble with that is you can't really start another film because anything else would be an anti-climax after that terrific ending at the New Year's Eve party.

Intellectuals have a habit of dismissing Rom-Coms as "entertainment" rather than "art". But just look at Billy Crystal's final speech and tell me it's not great writing:

"I love that you get cold when it's 71° outside. I love that it takes you an hour and a half to order a sandwich. I love that you get this little crinkle above your nose when you look at me like I'm nuts. I love that when I've spent the day with you, I can still smell your perfume on my clothes, and I love that you are the last person I want to talk to before I go to sleep at night

"And it's not because I'm lonely, and it's not because it's New Year's Eve. I came here tonight because when you realise that you want to spend the rest of your life with somebody, you want the rest of your life to start As Soon As Possible."

So I snuggled down in the big sleeping bag in the coffin - and once you've wrestled yourself into that, it's going to take a lot to get you out.

But then, the night promised to be very settled - just like the day - with the boat storming across a pretty much flat sea and a chagrined Eric running the show.

If I was going to have anything to write about tomorrow, I had better have a pretty good dream tonight.

I didn't know it at the time, but this was going to be a marathon of a night. I went to bed at 9.30p.m. remember?

When do you think I got up? 10.50a.m: 13 hours 20 minutes!

Yes, it's ridiculous, I know. But think about it. It was freezing cold in the cabin (but very warm in the Extreme Range sleeping bag). I could tell by the motion that nothing had changed. What was I going to do if I got up?

But I could make sure I had some dreams to write about.

At 0458, I recorded this on my phone:

"Looked at Navionics on the phone. 5.9 kts in the right direction. Gentle rocking and faint rushing noise (here, there was a 15-second gap when I appeared to fall asleep, before continuing) … you might almost think the boat is becalmed because there's so little swell."

0500: "Teddy bear chocolates and something to do with Government statements."

Heaven knows what that was about - although I do have a very clear memory of the chocolates: Filled with coconut like a Bounty bar - just shaped like a teddy bear with a little smiling face. What it had to do with government statements, I have no idea.

0456 Woke up at about 4.45. Thought: I don't need to get out of bed, don't need to pee like an old man waking up in the night or anything like that. Thought: I'll go back to sleep and dream about Hampshire Hospital.

Ah yes, Hampshire Hospital. It's a bit of a shame about that - it was a very powerful dream and I dictated a full report in the small hours. However, it seems I never pressed the "record" button, so the trials of trying to find my way on my Brompton bicycle across the sandy paths of some common I seem to remember from my schooldays in Surrey will have to wait for a return visit.

What I do remember is stopping everyone I passed and asking the way - and they all turned out to be the same person. Eventually, this person became really quite angry… which in some way was connected to the government statement and the teddy bear chocolates. But you'll have to work that out for yourself.

Stop Press: I found the recording two days later, and I think it would be rather fun, after you've read the last two paragraphs about it going missing, to find out what was so wonderful about it that should cause all this fuss.

Here it is:

I spent the night trying to find Hampshire Hospital. It seems that I had retired, and I was going to write a blog about being an old man. There's a wonderful book called Diary of an Old Man, which eulogises the trivia of the small life of an anonymous old man living in a seedy boarding house somewhere anonymous like Hainault or Epping. I seemed to have the idea of updating this as a blog, *which I suppose is what the Oldmansailing blog turned out to be.*

However, it seems that this is not nearly as easy as writing a blog on a boat where there's always something happening - always something to do. I was living at home, and every day everyone went off to school and Tamsin went off to work, and I was just sort of left.

First of all, I wandered all round the house and fused all the lights in the downstairs loo, and there was smoke and the smell of burning, and I was worried that I had set fire to the house. Then I discovered the most wonderful window that I didn't know about. It was curved, and you could slide it up, not like a sash window that just goes up and down. This one slid back over your head and made a lovely little balcony where you could sit in the sun.

But after ten minutes of sitting in the sun, I thought: "Well, I've sat in the sun, so now what am I going to do?"

I had my little Brompton bicycle and, for some reason, it was absolutely vital that I go to Hampshire Hospital. Everyone said: "Well, you'll have to take the train or the bus or something."

You see, I didn't realise that Hampshire Hospital was about 40 miles away, so I set off on my bicycle - and proceeded to have a series of adventures, many of which concerned the same man who had become so cross about being asked the way. This time, he refused to tell me. I never discovered why, exactly. I think he considered I was just wasting my time and everybody else's by asking directions to a hospital 40 miles away.

I kept coming to the same series of road junctions, some of them involving farm tracks, some connecting motorways, and the signposts didn't help.

Then I was at a supermarket - actually, I was cycling around inside the supermarket and upsetting everybody. There was a family who had just got a brand new dog off Amazon, and the dog was behaving atrociously, and I went and asked them the way to Hampshire Hospital - which made them cross as well.

But I managed to mollify them by saying: "Oh, we had a dog off Amazon. He was absolutely wonderful."

05.10. Woke up to the sound of a sail banging and the boat suspiciously upright. Had we gybed? Thought I ought to get up and see what was happening. Nothing was happening. Eric looked at me accusingly. I think he's back to his old self.

0520. Finally got up to pee. Checked the instruments: 753 miles to Inishtrahull. Batteries still at 88% even with the wind charger off. Back to bed. Didn't want another confrontation with Eric.

0632. In a car reciting the Air Force motto. *Without pain, there is no brotherhood* (is that a translation of *Per Adua ad Astra?*) Meryl

Streep sitting next to me. We were discussing Lottie and the scoreboard.

Lottie was about ten in this dream. When I'm awake, she's 24. Anyway, she was about ten and most upset because her parents were divorced, and she was spending the weekend with her father. It seemed that somebody else was her father, which lets me off the hook. She was going to be scoring at a cricket match between Eton and Cheltenham College (isn't that a girls' school?) She was the scorer and supposed to bring the scoreboard.

For those unfamiliar with the game of cricket. The scoreboard is traditionally an enormous rickety structure about thirty feet high and on little iron wheels. The scorers (one from each team) climb up stairs inside - even more rickety. Halfway up there is a sort of window without glass where they sit side by side and observe, writing down every run, every over, every wicket, etc. With them will be the tallyman, provided by the home side, whose job it is to crank ancient wooden handles to display the score for all the people watching from the boundary. Now you know.

Meryl and I agreed that her father should drive Lottie back to her mother's house in Kent to get the scoreboard - there would still be time if they started now.

0637: Rolled down my woolly hat to keep out the light. Don't need to get up because it'll just be another day of flying along between six and seven knots in the right direction, so I might as well stay in bed and make sure I record all these dreams.

"But will anyone really want to read this rubbish," I asked myself aloud.

And replied to myself: "It doesn't matter. Just record it all, and then you can throw it all out at the end if it's no good."

I was having this discussion with myself when I thought: "Is this part of a dream or isn't it?" I still had the hat rolled down, so it was dark, and I really had no idea.

I still haven't.

0648. It's so difficult to remember these things now because they're coming so fast. This one was Meryl Streep again, and I was saying that I didn't need to record any more because it really was rubbish now.

And she said: "No, you must. You absolutely must. This is what people want to know."

So, God help me, we were driving along in a people carrier and Rowan Atkinson was sitting on somebody's lap. There was a good reason for this because the car was fitted with a commode under Rowan Atkinson's seat. So, when another passenger went to use it, Atkinson calmly sat back down - on his lap.

I think he must have been in character as Mr Bean.

0723: Now I was driving, and I was having trouble moving my feet on the pedals. Tamsin asked: "Would you like me to drive?"

I said "Yes" and we swapped over and I was thinking: "Oh God, I must be getting old."

I know that was a dream because there's nothing wrong with my feet, and I'm damn sure I'm not getting old!

0738: Anchored in Walton Backwaters, and there were these lovely little birds - very colourful and each with two or three chicks. Tamsin came walking across the island, which was made entirely of mussel shells. She told me to bring my shorts but not to bring any comics.

I said: "Why would I bring comics. I haven't read a comic in years - not since Owen was addicted to The Beano.

0825. I'm a doctor. But I'm driving a taxi and I'd got to where I needed to go, so I was trying to find somewhere to dump it. Suddenly, somebody got in the back, and I had to explain why I was a doctor driving a cab.

0839: Samsara sank in a pond in Suffolk. I had her on a mooring, but somebody offered me a lift ashore in a dinghy, so I dropped the mooring and went with them. When I came back, she was aground at the edge of the pond. So, I pushed her off - she was only small. Then I sat astride her (she must have been very small) and pumped her out by sticking my hand down through the little hatch that model boats used to have.

There was somebody on the shore and I asked them: "How do I get her craned out?" and they said: "Go and see Mrs Thingummy (it was a triple-barrelled name). She'll help you."

In all, there were 20 recordings, but some were incoherent. In others, I seemed to have gone back to sleep. Some were just plain boring (even more boring). I mean, what would you make of 0855 and: "I was getting better and better boats and almost had a reputation for competence. I still had Meryl Streep with me, though."

Day 37

Thursday 22nd May 2025.
51°27.045'N 26°09.112'W.
Wind: SW6. Barometer: 1022.
Day's Run: 130M.
Total: 4,345.
Average: 117.4.
Distance to Destination: 860M.
ETA: 7.3 days = 29th May.

It's true. You can have too much of a good thing. Sleep, for instance. I usually have an hour's kip in the afternoon - you never know what the night is going to bring.

But I set the alarm for 1hr 8mins (what difference would it make? And then woke with the motion and a sail flapping and saw I still had 17 minutes to go. So, I set it for 20 minutes … and when that alarm went off, I pressed "reset". Total: 1hr 40mins - and after the hibernation of last night as well…

I leapt out of bed and started giving myself a serious talking to (I could hear sniggering from the cockpit).

And Eric was right. Things were getting out of hand. For one thing, the speed readout on the plotter seemed to be stuck somewhere between 7.5 and 8.5kts. For *Samsara*, that is seriously fast. Exhilarating, certainly, but producing a very uncomfortable motion and hard on the helmsman - and I didn't want to go through Tuesday again. She would be much better under twin headsails. It wouldn't make that much difference to the speed.

Twin headsails is the Tradewind Rig. It's a bit of a palaver to set up, but if you can be sure of a following wind for the next two weeks, then it's worth it.

Well, I have a forecast for a following wind for the next three days - that's as far as I reckon you can trust a forecast in these latitudes, but it would mean I could cook without dumping the noodles all over the chart table. Also, that following wind could well be blowing at 30 knots, and while I am proud of the gooseneck screw, I think it deserves some consideration.

I liked to think this was going to be a slick operation - just as reefing is now a slick operation (I get enough practice).

Unfortunately, I don't get a lot of practice with the Tradewind Rig. The last time I was "running down the trades" was two years ago. So, I decided to start with a proper "harbour stow" of the mainsail - and I must say it does look good - all pulled back and flaked with all seven sail ties. That mainsail's not going anywhere.

The next bit wasn't so easy. It involved two headsails, two booms, and ten control lines - halyards, sheets, guys and downhauls - and all of them have to be rigged in the right order or something is bound to get the wrong side of something else.

It did.

So everything had to come down again.

Honestly, I went on deck at 3.30 and didn't get back again until 6.45. I'm not very good at remembering boring procedures. I put it down to what I politely call "The Condition" (if you don't know about this, see my book *Faster, Louder, Riskier, Sexier: Learning to Love ADHD*).

On this occasion, I forgot how many turns to give the removable inner forestay bottle screw to lengthen it just the right amount to reach the eyebolt. I forgot that the lazy headsail sheet goes inboard of the stay - and that the staysail halyard needs to be inboard of the headsail sheet.

There were other omissions as well (not putting a stopper knot on the sheet - that sort of thing. There was a lot of traipsing back and forth between the foredeck and the cockpit - and jolly hard work it was too.

But worth it in the end.

When eventually, I got back below and looked at the plotter, we were doing between 6.5 and 7.5kts - and now, here I am sitting with the first beer (believe me, there are going to be two tonight) and the motion is hardly noticeable.

It can blow as hard as it likes (as long as it's from behind). All I have to do is roll up the headsail, and the staysail will continue to pull us at a steady seven knots, reducing that 30kt "red wind" to a modest 23kts - and doing no harm at all to the ETA.

*

I dreamed that I fell overboard. This had to happen sometime - I give so much thought to it, the subject was bound to crop up in the subconscious.

However, I think it may have had something to do with the *Singlehanded Tips, Thoughts & What-have-you* book. Obviously, it had a section on jackstays and harnesses. My jackstays are in the lazarette, and generally I only wear a harness when removing the mainsail, which involves standing up at the mast and using both hands above my head.

Naturally, the book advocated anything that would keep the singlehanded sailor attached to the boat. One point I found interesting was that the aft ends of the jackstays should be far enough forward to avoid the man overboard getting towed *behind* the boat - since nobody can pull themselves up a tether against a five-knot flow of water.

There were interviews with people who had fallen overboard and lived to tell the tale - they all seemed to have fallen over the lee side and either scrambled back when the boat dipped her rail again or been washed back by the next wave.

In my dream, it was rather different. I seem to have been pitched off the foredeck and went in head-first, turning a somersault underwater and bobbing up facing the other way.

Two things I remember. One was saying: "So that's it, then." After all, I have known for a long time that this is my most likely end - and, come to that, the one that I would choose. Much better to drown falling off your boat than fade away painfully and embarrassingly in some awful care home - because they are all awful, no matter how much they cost or how nice the gardens and oppressively cheerful the staff.

Also, *The Perfect Storm,* Sebastian Junger's exhaustively researched book about the loss of the fishing boat Andrea Gail off the coast of Massachusetts in 1991, suggests that drowning is not unpleasant. Apparently, just before the end, the victim experiences a great rush of euphoria for some reason. The evidence comes from people who were revived against all the odds.

But in the dream, I decided that what I really wanted was one last look at my boat sailing away from me into the sunset. So, I started paddling with my hands to turn myself around. I was in the middle of doing this when I thought back to that moment when I was in mid-air between foredeck and sea. The vision was filled with flapping harness tethers against a background of top-of-the-range red and white Gore-Tex foul-weather gear.

Mine's not like that. Mine is cheap blue and yellow Guy Cotten (with porous knees).

I stopped paddling and said to myself: "You don't suppose this is all a dream…"

So, I opened my eyes and found myself looking straight up through the central hatch to the same grey sky I'd been looking at for the past three days. It appeared that I would live to sail another day.

Given that I have been spared (as my grandmother used to say), I suppose I shouldn't complain. But I am getting a bit fed up with 15°C and 88% humidity - and a uniformly grey sky and visibility of less than a mile.

Everything in the cabin is clammy. I try to sit on the cushion the same way every time, so that one side remains clammy and the other dry. But since the cushion looks the same on both sides, I may have got it mixed up, and now when I stand up, my trousers stick to me.

There are only two decent teabags left before I have to broach the "black tea" from the Chinese supermarket - and the Nutella jar is at a critical level.

On the plus side, according to the ETA calculations, I can afford half an onion a day. I feel I am entitled to this since the carrots are finished.

There is plenty of beer, and at last the fridge - at 11°C - is colder than the 15°C cabin temperature. Even though the sky remains a relentless grey day after day, the new Lithium batteries stay above 85%. Admittedly, I'm not using electricity for cooking while I use up the last of the gas - but nor am I running the wind charger because the solar panels seem capable of supplying all the instruments, lights and watermaker - not to mention Eric's 24-hour shifts at the helm.

One other thing - and most importantly: It looks as though I will have a following wind all the way into the North Channel. There were times in the night when I wondered whether I should reef - I was seeing 28kts on the clock - which, added to a boat speed of seven, put us into "Full Gale" territory. But then it would drop down to 22kts, and I would think we could manage, especially if I lopped 10° off the course to stop the headsail flapping.

When I started the day (at a respectable 0730), I did reef - and put the 10° back. We're averaging better than six knots in the right direction. Best of all, Windy says I can look forward to at least a couple more days of this.

Day 38

> Friday 23rd May 2025.
> 52°33.666'N 22°49.213'W.
> Wind: W7. Barometer: 1019.
> Day's Run: 140M.
> Total: 4,495M.
> Average: 118M.
> Distance to Destination: 719M.
> ETA: 6.1 days = 29th May.

Two red bush tea bags left. No Twinings English Breakfast. Two kilos of coffee beans, but the grinder won't charge. Plenty of Maggi stock cubes.

Six days to go.

So, the quandary is whether to drink the two redbush bags as if there's no tomorrow or keep them for a special occasion - arriving in the Irish Sea… arriving in the Isle of Man…

Or, to try the very suspect Rika's China Black Tea Blend $4 for 100 bags (and I bought two boxes). I have been suspicious ever since I saw that they also offered Spearmint, Lemongrass, Camomile and Mint flavours. At least if I tried it, I would know where I stood.

I broached one of the boxes, stored in a Tupperware behind the sultanas (teabags loose in a cardboard box do not fare well on a small boat. Always buy teabags in individual foil wrapping.)

Unless you drink that much tea, of course…

Anyway, I fished one out from the other 99, read the label: They were packed in Panama by the Wong corporation, and the instructions were all in Spanish. I now know the word for "enjoy". I poured over boiling water. I waited 3-5 minutes. I was all ready to "enjoy".

But I didn't. Shall we say that Chinese black tea is an acquired taste - rather like green tea except, well… black.

I added sugar and coffee whitener, which works well with Mr Twining's products, but this was not the same at all. I was going to be reduced to a third of a red bush tea bag a day - or, alternatively, a whole one every three days.

I was about to pour it down the sink, when I thought to add honey. This works well with red bush (to my mind, honey works well with anything.)

And I can report that it works well with Chinese Black Tea - you just need enough of it.

I was about to write that the voyage may be a success after all, when I remembered something else: Those little black bugs? The ones that got into the rice? (And everywhere else).

Since the temperature dropped like a stone when we hit the Canadian border and then dropped some more overnight, they haven't been a problem. All the same, it is not easy to forget them - especially when one turns up in a mug that hasn't been used for a few weeks.

I was rummaging in the "packets and jars locker". Packets and jars go together like a wink and a smile because the packets become the packing to stop the jars crashing together and breaking. One of the packets was chia seeds.

Chia seeds are tremendously good for you and, for some reason, are available absolutely everywhere in Central America. I add about a third of a packet to the oats container for my breakfast "Bircher muesli" (or, as it is at the moment, Gulf Stream Breakfast).

Somehow, I had forgotten all about them for several weeks, so you would think I would be pleased to see the wholesome little black specks sprinkled through my morning Tupperware.

Not when they look exactly like another infestation getting started.

And Eric still keeps on steering. I don't know why I should have doubted him - it's just that I have had such a long and frustrating history with autopilots that it is difficult to summon up the confidence he deserves. But he is considerably more expensive and sophisticated than any I have had before, so maybe I'm being unfair.

All the same, we are now trailing the long warp in a bight from the stern cleats. It helps keep the boat straight and should ease the strain on Eric's circuits and bushes.

"Just keep going till we get there!"

Actually, just keep going until the Aries gets fixed. It's like driving on the spare tyre and hoping that doesn't get a blow-out as well.

While we're discussing the crew, I cannot understand that when I had the Aries in pieces all over the cabin and was trying to fit bolts in holes which didn't match, I never thought to consult Chiefy.

I have written about Chiefy elsewhere, and he has a whole blog post to himself, which you can find with the search box. But briefly, Chiefy is the teddy bear who sat on my father's bed during his final illness. He was given to me by my sister as a mascot. I can hardly get rid of him, no matter how unsentimental I claim to be.

Chiefy has become a feature aboard *Samsara* - my granddaughter Phoebe wouldn't dream of stepping through the companionway without immediately checking on Chiefy.

Whenever I find myself at a loss over anything mechanical, I have only to give his foot a tweak and say: "Come on, Chiefy. Get to it!" and somehow, miraculously, either the answer comes to me, or the recalcitrant machine starts working of its own accord.

Partly to remind me (and partly to give him the status he deserves), he now has his own tool kit.

On my previous Rival, *Largo,* back in the 80s, there was a little locker down at floor level in the galley that was the ready-use tool box. All the screwdrivers and mole grips that you use every day were in there, ready to hand.

I don't have such a locker on *Samsara* and so, every time I want a screwdriver, I have to root out "Toolbox Number 1" (there's a bit of tape with its number stuck on the lid - like Toolbox Number 2 and Toolbox Number 3).

But now Chiefy has two screwdrivers (standard and Philips) and a pair of pliers tucked into the shock cord with him beside the navigator's seat.

I've never seen him look so proud.

*

After all those long nights with nothing happening - unless you count the subconscious, tonight is nothing if not busy. Waking at half past two, everything seemed ominously quiet. There was no creaking of sheets under strain - no rushing water. Eventually, I managed to manoeuvre an arm out of the sleeping bag - which, believe me, is an achievement - especially in the coffin. The phone was in the fiddle above the bunk, and Navionics showed we were down to two knots.

On any other trip, I might think I could wait for the morning, but that might be six hours away. If I could find another knot, I could be six miles ahead by then - two knots would be twelve!

I got up and looked out. Sure enough, the apparent wind was down to 18kts - still a stiff breeze, but nothing like the near-gale that had been blowing when I went to bed. The long warp was still trailing astern - now just slowing us down. I hauled that into the aft end of the cockpit and got an extra half a knot.

The problem was the scrap of headsail, which was really doing nothing. Poled out on the leeward side, it needed a much closer sheeting angle - and then I could unroll some more. Interestingly, I was consciously careful as I made my way up to the foredeck: All this discussion about harnesses and tethers and jackstays - the accounts of people falling over and climbing back aboard, all served to put me in mind of treading water and watching *Samsara's* stern light disappearing below the waves.

Sitting here writing about it at four o'clock in the morning, I have just checked to see that I had switched on the masthead tricolour - and found I hadn't. Now I have a special "tricolour" alarm set for nine o'clock every night…

Without the pole and the sail now rolled out to the first reef, we are averaging four-and-a-half knots - although we were doing better than that when I sat down with the laptop and a flask of black tea with a slug of rum. Do I really have to go out and put it all back again?

The urgency is because I have this idea that if I can get the new cooker delivered to the Isle of Man, I may not have to pay VAT - which on a price of £2,900 is worth considering.

However, I still have to sell the old one. It's too big to take with me. So, I need enough time in Douglas while still leaving three days to get to Falmouth for the 50th anniversary celebrations of the Azores and back Race. Can you believe it is 38 years since I did my first one!

*

Well, we're certainly getting there in a hurry. It's just monstrously uncomfortable.

At 0930, I woke to a tremendous flapping and found the wind up to 28kts, and the starboard sheet winch had let go. Eric hadn't been able to bring her back on course and had gone into "standby" mode - which means he turns his back on the situation and stands at the rail with his arms folded and a sour expression on his face.

Of course, I had to get all kitted up, which was pretty unpleasant, what with the knees of my trousers still being sopping wet - and, I noticed, wet all the way up the inside seams as far as the crotch. But I couldn't be dealing with that now. I went and sorted everything out and got her sailing again. I'd serviced both winches before I left, but that doesn't mean anything. Anyway, this time I put the tail of the sheet on a cleat.

It took so little time that I was still thinking of wet trousers when I got down again - and decided it was time to move on to a clean pair (a dry pair). The "seriously wet pair", which has been hanging up for two days and doing nothing but contribute to the 86% humidity went into the wardrobe locker with socks, long johns and underwear which, I now realise, I have been wearing since May 4th - a full three weeks. I said this was going to be a voyage of records.

Since the cold is now the Number One enemy rather than damp (it is 16°C in the cabin, but I'm horrified to find I'm getting used to it), I am now wearing the Gill "Base Layer" which claims to "wick" moisture away from the skin. I was rather impressed - until I sat down.

Adding to the general level of discontent, this change in wind direction has resulted in an unusually lumpy sea which, coming largely from the beam, periodically crashes over the boat and finds all those little gaps and crevices and lets in the drips which… well, I think you get the picture.

Apparently, the wind is due to back sometime around midday, although it will still be Force 7. At least it will be going my way.

Day 39

> Saturday, 24th May 2025.
> 53°16.608'N 19°35.067'W.
> Wind: W7. Barometer: 1007.
> Day's Run: 125M.
> Total: 4610M.
> Average: 118.2.
> Distance to Destination: 595M.
> ETA: 5 days = 29th May.

At last the wind backed, so now we're charging along with just a double-reefed headsail, averaging 5.8kts with the wind aft of the beam. There have even been some flashes of sunshine - enough to bring the batteries up from 70% to 73%, despite the drain of instruments and autopilot - why did I ever doubt Lithium?

More to the point, I have opened the main hatch and the forehatch to get a flow of air going through the boat and, almost immediately, the humidity has dropped from 86% to 78%. There is a risk in this because we are still taking water on the side decks - I haven't opened the centre hatch because I'm sitting right under it and I've already had to buy one new screen for the laptop because it got soaked.

A more pressing problem is that I've just made myself a Maggi drink - three little cubes in an insulated flask with boiling water. It's lovely to sip, but you have to be careful in case the boat lurches and you end up with a scalding mouthful. I've found the only thing to do is to spit it back as soon as possible. It's a bit like the underwear - I've only myself to offend.

*

Belay that, as they say. It turns out this is not going to be the racing finish I predicted. Instead, the "orange wind" the Windy app had predicted for the weekend - well, deep orange, it must be admitted - up to 30kts (Force 7), we've now got a consistent 36kts, which is Force 8 and definitely "red wind".

It was OK to begin with. We were flying along. Then the reefed headsail kept getting taken aback because there were some pretty big waves, and Eric just couldn't cope. So, I poled out the headsail. Then I streamed the long warp. Then I took the pole down again. Then I tried just a tiny scrap of headsail.

Nothing seemed to work. We would have been all right with the Aries - but Eric is just too slow to react, with the result that every ten minutes or so, he would go to "standby". Somehow, I couldn't face a whole evening of this - and what about the night?

Well, you can tell where this is going, can't you? In the end, I went and dragged out the SeaBrake. I have a theory that I could let go of one end of the long warp and stream the drogue from the other quarter before taking in the warp - at least that would give me some stability during the changeover process. But when it came to it, I was too scared of them getting tangled. So, I hauled in the warp and, of course, that meant we were back to an erratic course, and the next thing you know, a wave breaks into the cockpit - all over me.

While all this was all going on. the bimini started coming adrift so I had to stand up on the aft deck and tie that down again.

And then began the process of experimenting to see if we could keep to the course. It took the best part of an hour. At one point, the pole went up again - and then came down again. The headsail got bigger - and then smaller.

An hour later, we're sort of on course and certainly under control. I don't think dinner is going to be interrupted, and I'm looking forward to an undisturbed night.

It's just that we're not going very fast - average speed is 3.1kts. Who cares. I'm awarding myself a second beer since the six o'clock beer signals the start of the evening, and this one certainly didn't get started.

Until now, that is. Now Bob Dylan doesn't think twice on Spotify, and I've found a jar of Cajun spices.

*

Yes. Well, not as undisturbed as I had hoped.

I did get a bit of warning. I was about to start dinner - I had the garlic in my hand - when there was a great rushing noise and a solid waved dumped itself in the cockpit - and, of course, squirted through the cracks all round the companionway. I find this singularly unfair since, when I measured it, I didn't allow for the thickness of the varnish, and it fits so tightly that, sometimes I have to get the rubber hammer to free it.

But not tightly enough to keep out the water, apparently.

It didn't get me, but it did thoroughly soak the chart table, so dinner was taken on the lee berth.

And then it happened again as I was about to start washing up. I think they call it a pre-rinse.

But at least the waves were coming from the aft quarter as they're supposed to. The boat was riding well, and we were actually making some progress, averaging 3.3kts in the right direction. I went to bed feeling quite pleased, all things considered.

And then, at four o'clock, there was an enormous bang and I opened my eyes just in time to see things flying over my head.

Oh no, I thought. It's The Canaries all over again - another knockdown. But no, it was just that the electric toothbrush charger and a jar of mixed herbs shooting from port to starboard - the mixed herbs smashing its plastic lid so that now the whole place smells like Nigella's kitchen.

More worrying was why? A bang like that and things flying about suggest a wave arriving beam-on instead of at an angle. Beam-on is dangerous. Beam-on is how you get rolled.

I got up and looked. Sure enough, Eric had gone into "standby" mode again.

So, I got dressed up and went and set him straight. This time, as an afterthought, I pressed the "wind" button and - hallelujah, it worked. Now, he could really do his job.

But only for an hour. This was no good at all. We had another 24 hours to go like this. There must be some way to stop the bow coming up into the wind - after all, you would think that a boat left to her own devices with a darned great drogue off the stern, would weather-cock downwind.

So, I started experimenting again - tiller lashed to weather. Tiller lashed a-lee. Tiller swinging free. Less sail. Even less sail. More sail. No sail.

And that's what worked in the end: Running with a bare pole and Eric steering by the wind to keep it on the quarter.

He does seem to keep the helm sawing back and forth a lot. I just hope he can keep going.

Me? I went back to bed, listening to the main halyard tapping, the mugs clinking quietly in their rack and marvelled that whatever happens, the whisky bottle never seems to move.

Meanwhile, we head for Galway at 2.3kts.

Day 40

> Sunday 25th May, 2025.
> 56°37.847'N 17°18.425'W.
> Wind: W7. Barometer: 1011.
> Day's Run: 84M.
> Total: 4,694M.
> Average: 117.3M.
> Distance to Destination: 511M.
> ETA: 4.4 days = 29th May.

Actually, things didn't work out quite as I'd hoped. Somewhere in the middle of the night, there was another great crash and the sound of heavy water running off the deck. Also, it squirted in through the companionway once more, soaking the chart table and upending the washing-up basket onto the floor and smashing a cereal bowl I don't like anyway. Now there are only three to go until I can get some new ones.

By three o'clock, things had quietened down considerably. The wind dropped right away, and Eric was grinding endlessly backwards and forwards. I'm so anxious to keep him happy that I just had to get up and pull out more sail - even if it was raining.

Then I thought: "What's the point of doing that with a ruddy great drogue hanging out the back?"

So, the SeaBrake would have to come in - but the long warp was still piled up at the aft end of the cockpit. If I was going to do things right (and I'm always reminding myself what a good idea that is) I should put the warp away first. It has to be flaked into two supermarket "bags for life" and then piled one on top of another in the port cockpit locker (where the top bag falls off unless the SeaBrake cable is in there to wedge it.

Furling the headsail just about stopped the boat. I was congratulating myself on hauling in the whole 37m of rope, 10m of 10mm chain and finally thing itself - all without benefit of a winch - when I discovered why it had come home so easily.

It was broken.

It turns out that 24 hours on the back of a boat of less than ten metres, in a minor gale (I never saw the windspeed over 38kts, and mostly it was around 30-35), is too much for a SeaBrake.

The circle or rigging wire had snapped. This is what holds the larger chamber open until it is folded in on itself by the force of water. This is serious stuff - 6mm rigging wire. Moreover, each of the four webbing straps had chafed through the fabric. I took photographs and will write to SeaBrake.

Meanwhile, there was nothing to be done about it out here. I had less than 500 miles to go. With any luck, I wouldn't need it again.

We still had a following wind at about 20kts, so I set the headsail with the second reef. Eric said something about "bloody time too" and, as a reward for "doing it right", I brought breakfast forward by two hours.

Hardly was I back into bed when the headsail started banging all over the place, Eric was grinding (I couldn't tell whether it was the drive unit or his teeth), and the wind was down to less than 10kts.

I went through the same argument as before - "doing things right" versus staying in a warm bed. From the dripping hatch, it appeared to be still raining. The drips landing on the starboard berth - which is why I am still in the port one, even though it's the "uphill" side.

Anyway, I got into my clammies again and went out and re-set the mainsail and boomed out the headsail and wondered about where to go.

Yesterday's forecast had a very precise area of calm. It might be quite easy to avoid if I acted now. I treated myself (and Mr Musk) to a couple of quid's worth of Internet and logged onto Windy.

Yes, if I got going now, by midday, I should have 20kts on the quarter and a straight run to Inishtrahull.

By the time I had dealt with all of that, spent a long time standing in the hatch looking at the imperceptibly-lightening greyness and cogitated about storm tactics, it seemed like breakfast time again.

Obviously, I couldn't just make a Gulf Stream Breakfast like that - it takes a good ten hours.

But I could make hot porridge.

Now there was a thought - with sultanas and coffee whitener and brown sugar. I started salivating at the very thought of it.

And my word, on a miserable cold morning with the hatch dripping and the drips soaking into a kapok cushion positioned right beside you for that very purpose, hot porridge doesn't half hit the spot.

So, now I have to decide what to do about the SeaBrake. Obviously, I shall write to the company in Australia and send them a photo. But I can't think what they could say to restore my faith in its ability to withstand a proper storm. The plaudits from people like John Sanders and Robin Knox-Johnston were all for the previous model - made of rigid plastic with spring-loaded flaps. That would be a nightmare to stow on a small boat. Presumably, that's why they came up with the fabric version.

Most recently, I see that Sanders has used a car tyre. I saw a picture where he had it lashed to the guardrails - and it was a big one because it stuck up above the top rail. And think how heavy a car tyre is to manhandle back aboard?

The generally accepted solution is the Jordan Series Drogue, and while I have catalogued its drawbacks, there seems to be no doubt that it does work.

One of the things I liked about the SeaBrake was the way it would hold the bow up to the wind when hove-to, because heaving-to cuts down the drift dramatically. Not only can you keep off a lee shore for longer, but the storm will pass over you more quickly - after all, the longer you have to endure it by running with it, the more likelihood of things going wrong.

Yes, I can see it all: I would have it set off the bow while lying hove-to, but if the storm became too violent, I would transfer it to the stern the same way I did with the SeaBrake.

Or maybe the SeaBrake would be OK off the bow with the boat hove-to and hardly moving. Maybe it was being towed at four knots that broke it. I could try it on a really short line so there was no chance of it getting tangled with the JSD while I deployed that off the stern (and of course, since we wouldn't be moving, that would be so much easier to do). It's worth a try - in fact, when it comes to the laborious task of recovering the JSD, wouldn't that be so much easier if I hove-to first? Nobody seemed to mention that.

The series drogue is jolly expensive, of course, but I believe you can buy the cones ready-made and splice them into the line yourself - not a bad idea because they can suffer in a really bad and prolonged blow. Then at least you'd know how to replace them.

Meanwhile, it's good to be making progress again - six knots bang and on target - even if it is still raining.

Day 41

> Monday 26th May, 2025.
> 54°01.711'N 15°27.025'W.
> Wind" W4. Barometer: 1005.
> Day's Run: 70M.
> Total: 4,764M.
> Average: 116.2M.
> Distance to Destination: 441M.
> ETA: 3.8 days = 30th May.

How things can change in a heartbeat! When I logged on for the weather forecast at eight o'clock this morning, I wondered whether I should collect the emails and see who was on WhatsApp. But that's something I do at midday, so I decided I would go through the whole ritual when the proper time came.

Remember that at eight, it was all clear through to Inishtrahull?

By midday, out of nowhere, a sudden vicious and fast-moving low was shooting like a cannonball right across the little blue logo denoting "my position".

I looked again. I checked. I worked the timeline. There was no doubt. This thing would hit just as I was approaching the waypoint. And this wasn't the modest gale that had destroyed the SeaBrake. This was "blue wind".

We haven't talked about "blue wind". I only took you as far as "red wind" (30-40kts).

Blue wind is 40 - 50kts.

And an increase from 40 to 50 isn't like the difference between driving at 40 miles an hour and driving at 50 miles an hour. With wind speeds, there is a complicated squaring of the arithmetic as there is with the Richter Scale of earthquakes. This means that 41 knots is an awful lot worse than 40 knots - and you don't want to know about 49 knots…

This was serious. It is just not sensible to venture into the confined and rock-strewn waters of an inhospitable coast like north-west Ireland in anything but clement weather.

I had chosen the North Channel into the Irish Sea because it was shorter. Now it was clear that I should do a sharp right turn and go in by the south - St George's Channel. I would still have a stiff breeze - but a good stiff sailing breeze, not survival conditions - and with a broken drogue.

I gybed and poled out the headsail once more, then came back below and looked at the chart. The new waypoint is The Bull - a lighthouse off the south west coast at the entrance to Bantry Bay. The change adds 84 miles to the route, but at the current average, that is a mere 17 hours.

We should be able to manage that if the "stiff breeze" can make up for the calms I might expect before the storm arrives (and, I hope, passes to the north of me).

Of course, nothing is certain in weather forecasting, and these violent and fast-moving lows can be notoriously capricious. Still, all I can do is act on the information I have - and maybe contribute a bit more to Mr Musk's billions with more frequent forecasts. At least if it does turn south, the Celtic Sea is a lot roomier than that narrow gap between Northern Ireland and Scotland.

At least it's stopped raining and the sun has come out. The air temperature may only be 15°C, but the hatches are open and the wind is blowing through.

*

Thinking about how to pay for a JSD (it's what the cognoscenti call the Jordan Series Drogue), the obvious economy is not to buy a ridiculously expensive GN electric cooker for £2,900.

I could get a cheap gas cooker for maybe £450 - and just not have any gas cylinders for it, but use it as a base for my little induction hob (maybe if I can get the measurements right - a twin hob). Then I could keep an electric toaster in the oven - it's not as if I'd have any other use for it.

As if that wasn't reason enough to be cheerful. I just went up to gybe. Since we're running, so this involves gybing the poled-out headsail, so more deck-work. I didn't have to fight my way into clammy oilskins for it. With Crocs on my feet, the indoor hat on my head, I'm not even going to complain about the cold. I did lose one of the pole uphauls up the mast, though. Not serious because I've got another, and I can't see the need for two poles before we get to Douglas.

*

Great mysteries of life Number 176: How do things on boats get fouled up when it is impossible for them to do so without human intervention?

I have just spent ten minutes on deck in 30kts re-threading the twing.

If you're not familiar with a twing, it is known - more prosaically - as a barber-hauler. But since that is equally unenlightening, I prefer "twing". It has a cute ring to it. If you want to be really boring and just want to know what it does, it is a stainless steel ring around the headsail sheet attached to a 5mm line, which can be controlled from the cockpit, pulling the ring down alters the angle of the sheet - an easier alternative than changing the position of the fairlead.

All of which is a lot of explanation considering it doesn't even begin to address what the thing had got up to. It was the wrong side of the guardrail. How did it do that?

Honestly, I haven't been near it for months, and the last time I had the sheets off was when? Well, I can't remember. Maybe not since the new sail arrived in 2023.

Yet, there was no doubt about it. Somebody had been interfering, and since I am the only one here (I don't really believe Eric is anything more than a collection of diodes and microprocessors), the only possible explanation is that the Twing did this by itself.

Maybe it is unhappy about being given a silly name.

*

Disaster! Absolute disaster! I sat down this morning to write an account of last night's events (many), and this manuscript wasn't waiting for me when I switched on.

Instead, under the title "Voyage #3 2.3.24" (there's still only one version despite having started it more than a year ago), I found something else entirely. If you must know, it was a plan of The Voyage numbers 4&5, together with distances and times.

But that is neither here nor there - literally, because I can't find that either, now I want it. But it doesn't matter, I've got several versions of that one because I keep changing my mind about it.

What I didn't have - and what was the major disaster - was the 66,000 or so words I had written so far about this voyage.

You can read about authors losing manuscripts. Kate Kerrigan left her all-but-completed *The Dress* in the back of a Dublin Taxi - and then didn't even dedicate the book to the driver who returned it. Instead, it's for "Niall, Leo and Tommo" - where's the feel-good story in that? Jilly Cooper famously left the only copy of *Riders* on a bus. She couldn't bear to start again from page one - well, not for fourteen years. Then there is the scene in Love Actually when Colin Firth watches his thriller-in-the-making blow into the pond.

Of course, I wasn't really worried. Computers never really forget everything. Many is the crook who thought he had deleted the incriminating evidence on his phone, only to have a hacker in a darkened room at Scotland Yard retrieve it. So, I knew that all I would have to do when I arrive is take the laptop to the local techie. I could just carry on with a new file.

But, I couldn't. I just sat here staring at the screen, thinking: "There's an archive somewhere. It's designed for people who change their minds a lot (guilty). You can retrieve an earlier version. I've done it myself (I'm sure I have)."

All I had to do was open up the "Finder" page - and just repeat what I'd done - fruitlessly - ten minutes ago. But it seemed the book was doomed. The first 66,000 words had gone AWOL. Now I would never complete it because I wouldn't be able to stop worrying about the beginning (and the middle…)

There was only one thing to do - go online and pose the question: "How to retrieve a lost Word document."

But first, I needed to know how much it would cost me in data. Mr Musk is charging 104,661 Colombian pesos for each gigabyte. It sounds frighteningly expensive, but the Colombians have had a bit of a tussle with inflation over the years, and 104,661 pesos turns out to be £1.86. I spent five minutes reading advice such as "Do a factory reset" and "reconfigure the network" - and then went and looked in the usual places one last time.

And there it was - the sentence about the Twing. Just as I'd left it. I can only think that it was saved on the cloud, and I was searching offline.

Once I was online again - and Starlink had initialised and stabilised, and established that "Starlink is determining alignment" and "optimizing connection", it seemed a bit of a waste to just log off again because I'd found what I was looking for - after all, there were plenty of other things that might be interesting...

Like the weather - again.

And sure enough, the Windy algorithm had changed its mind once more, and now it wasn't such a good idea to head for The Bull and St George's Channel after all. Oh, it would be all right when I got there, but first I had to get through about 50 miles of calms - whereas that vicious little low that was heading for Inishtrahull? That had decided to go and upset people in the Outer Hebrides instead. It wasn't even going to make much of a job of that, because the "blue wind" - the 40-50kt mayhem - was now somehow absent. I thought about this for a bit. I thought about the extra 84 miles. That could amount to a whole day. Imagine if that day, clawing my way up the Irish Sea turned out to be "Mad Sunday" in the TT and I missed it...

I turned left again and pointed the plotter at yesterday's waypoint - and put up the pole... and took it down again... and gybed this way and that...

And sometimes we averaged two knots and sometimes four, and Major Sharpe dispatched some more of Napoleon's forces and finished in extraordinarily bloodthirsty detail (it was my first of his Napoleonic adventures. I think I'll stick to Hornblower in future).

Casting around for something to do, I unscrewed the floor and brought up another dozen bottles of beer, replacing them with empties from the cockpit locker.

Only 348 miles to go.

*

It's May 28th. In Suffolk, people will be in their gardens, lighting up the barbecue, going to the beach. Yet here, 50 miles off the coast of Ireland, it's 15°C with a wind chill of -15°.

And I'm down to two teaspoons.

Teaspoons are important. I eat breakfast with a teaspoon because it takes longer that way. I need a teaspoon for digging into the peanut butter jar and then putting a dollop of honey on top (it used to be Nutella, but that's another grouse).

Still, mustn't complain - only 297miles to go. It would have been less, but the night before last, I set the alarm for two hours and then spent almost all of it going in the direction of Greenland at one knot with the mainsail backed on the preventer and not enough wind for the headsail to flap and wake me up. Last night I set one-hour alarms - and had to get up and gybe twice.

Not that I'm complaining…

On top of everything else, I spent the time on the Greenland detour having another stupid journalism dream. The worst of it was that I knew I was retired - in fact, I was on holiday visiting some far-flung but unspecified country. We stopped for coffee, and there was a man who had been pulled over in his Mercedes saloon for having 18 passengers.

Nobody could believe it: They were sitting on each others knees… I think there were three in the boot, folded up like socks stuffed into a sports bag.

The driver's name was Dar Trang. I know that was how it was spelled because I asked him - and then found I didn't have any paper to write it down.

There was great consternation in the crowd that I should be furnished with paper. Eventually, I took my stainless steel Space Pen (I used to be so proud of my Space Pen) - and found that it wouldn't write.

The same pandemonium, finding me a pen.

Finally, a man came walking down the street, having no idea what all the excitement was about. He was beaten to the ground and, without ceremony, relieved of his Bic biro. They had to prise it from his fingers.

I was not aware. By this time, I had been ushered into the back garden where there was a little stream with a bridge across it - a good place for an in-depth interview.

But we never got to that. I think I lost interest.

Do you blame me?

Day 43

> Wednesday 28th May 2025.
> 54°37.313'N 11°08.863'W.
> Wind SW4. Barometer: 1016.
> Day's Run: 78M.
> Total: 4,922M.
> Average: 114.5M.
> Distance to Destination: 287M.
> ETA: 2.5 days = 31st May.

Well, now it really is a race - that's the trouble with having weather forecasts. In the old days, I wouldn't have a care in the world - not knowing that at any moment the wind is going to leap from a gentle 15kts to a sporting 27kts… in an instant, according to the Windy app.

So, I had dinner early and washed up. The seaboots are waiting (already with the oilskin trousers rolled down round their ankles - the stout leather belt which I started wearing a couple of days ago and makes all the difference in the world - lives in right boot, ready to fight another day…)

The news is that I will have this hooley on my tail for 10 hours to get me to Inishtrahull and then a fair wind (green wind - 10-20kts) for the next 24 hours to blow me down to the Isle of Man. It's important that it works out like that. I must keep to the schedule because, after all of that, there is an extended period of calm (and remember I can't run the engine for more than five minutes). After the calm, it seems we're going to get headwinds; lots of strong headwinds.

But by then I will be in Douglas eating meals which other people have cooked (and more people will wash up), drinking beer out of glasses made of glass - and, of course, watching lunatics on motorcycles defying the laws of physics.

In the meantime, we're doing seven knots, so maybe the wind has arrived after all, and I just hadn't noticed.

Yes, the wind had arrived - honestly, all that stuff about: "I'd better go through the Celtic Sea and St George's Channel…"

I've just been looking at the track on Polarsteps and how much ground I lost. If I hadn't been sidetracked by having a weather forecast, I could have been another 20 miles further on.

Anyway, it all turned out to be pointless because I did get a gale in the north after all (I believe there was one in the south as well). There were times when it was blowing 40kts and I lost count of all the sail changes and the number of times I sat bouncing on the leeward berth trying to persuade my feet into the oilskin trousers and boots at the same time, and then hitching up the elasticated waistband and wondering why I never thought of buying some nice red banker's braces.

Then I would have to take the rubber hammer and bash at the handles of the washboard because all the water in the cockpit seems to swell the wood so that the whole thing jams solid. I must do something about that - at one point, I couldn't get back in. I'd gone out to reef (again) and put the board in behind me to stop the spray soaking the chart table - forgetting that if it sticks, you have to hammer the handles in an upwards direction - which, of course, you can't do from the cockpit because you are already in an upwards direction (i.e. standing in the cockpit, above the handles). Or to put it another way, you're stuck.

Fortunately, I've been trying for a year or more to get a piece of toughened glass to replace the Perspex window which shattered after six months. I still haven't managed it, and so I stuck some gaffer tape over the hole to keep the wind out. This turned out to be very convenient because all I have to do when I get stuck is rip off the tape, put my hand in the gap and give it a good yank.

Meanwhile, on the subject of trousers (I think we were on the subject of trousers), no sooner had I discovered that the stout leather belt was just what was needed than its buckle broke. Since then, I've been trying to hold them up with string. This is what you get for skipping lunch.

And if all that was going on in the daytime, you can imagine what happened at night. The wind always seems to blow harder at night - unless you have a calm, of course. A night-time calm is a study in stillness with silence and starlight that you can never experience on land.

I believe the people on the Titanic remarked on that.

Me, I had wind - all that night and all the next day. To begin with, I would get up and take the statutory four minutes to climb into the oilies and then go out and put the protesting Eric on standby (if he wasn't already) and tack the boat - or more likely gybe the boat. Then I would have to go down again to check the course on the plotter - and then back out again to mollify Eric and sit with him and see that he held the course.

And all of that would be repeated twenty minutes later, for the fact is that - conscientious though he is - Eric can't hold a candle to the Aries in strong winds: The harder it blows, the faster the boat goes - and the faster the boat goes, the harder the Aries works and the faster it corrects. There have been times, when digging into the cockpit lockers while underway, I have had to remind myself that if I were to get trapped awkwardly on the wrong side of the tiller, the forces of the wind, six knots through the water and a five-tonne boat could break my thigh without even raising an eyebrow.

So, inevitably, the moment would come - usually when I had peeled off the oilies, that I would have to put them back on again. Then I would go out into the cockpit in the rain and spray and decide it wasn't worth going below again. I would sit and watch the water and look at the sky and wonder why there were no birds - or maybe say to myself: "Oh look, there's a bird..."

Sure enough, Eric would tack again, or go into Standby, and I would have to take over - only this time, I wouldn't let him try again. I would hog the helm and pretend that it wasn't boring - or if it was, it was less boring than climbing in and out of clammy oilskins in a cabin that kept lurching and rolling with humidity in the high 80s.

And that was how I came to end up steering for two-and-a-half hours.

I didn't really have a lot of choice. The Aries couldn't do it. Eric wasn't going to do it - at least, not for more than five minutes at a time. Somebody had to be the responsible adult.

And so, as the wind fluctuated between 30 and 40 knots and Samsara shouldered her way along the coast of Northern Ireland, with rocks and bays and inlets and islands - Ballymastocker Bay, Carrickaveol Head - and, of course: Inishtrahull - I sawed at the tiller with one hand and then the other, and sometimes both, and thought that maybe wheel steering is not such a bad idea after all - even with 90m of multiplait hanging off the stern.

And sometimes I would hold the phone in one hand and thumb up the Windy app to see when all this was going to end. Actually, Windy insisted it was going to end at 0800... maybe 0900... possibly 1000 (possibly never).

Sometimes I would hear a roar behind me, and a wave would break into the cockpit.

I was in the cockpit.

It would hit me in the back and somehow contrive to trickle down my neck. The hand that was holding on would get a dollop up the sleeve. And it was bloody cold. I couldn't remember when I had been so cold - well, obviously I couldn't: For two years, my only concern had been finding some shade.

So instead, I thought about food. There wasn't any breakfast because I'd eaten that after Eric called me up (apparently because he was lonely).

The trouble was, I couldn't do any better. No matter how I tried to gybe the boat, she just wouldn't turn. I backed the headsail against its will. I even considered the engine. It was a remarkably long time before I realised that the water wasn't going past anymore - or at least if it was, it was going the other way: From stern to bow. Also, the waves weren't breaking over me as I sat with my back to the wind. They were breaking into my lap as I sat and watched the 90metres of line straining out astern, holding the full weight of the boat and 40kts of wind.

It is remarkable, sometimes, how long it takes the obvious to make an impression. But finally, I remembered the sensation: I was crossing the Stone Banks off Walton-on-the-Naze one pitch-black night in winter. The same sensation - one of not going anywhere…

That time, I had a lobster pot round the prop. This time, the 90metres of 14mm multiplait trailing astern had scooped up a buoy which must been anchored in the same spot for generations. Clearly, it would need an industrial salvage vessel to lift it.

But I didn't need to lift it did I? All I had to do was let go one end of the multiplait.

It whipped off the cleat and out of the fairlead, and *Samsara* accelerated from nought to eight knots in a faster than you could say "That was a bit of luck."

I fell across the tiller. It was vibrating, like it was a live thing.

I couldn't leave the cockpit. But, on the other hand, there was a pressing need (all that Chinese Black Tea). Some uncouth singlehanders will admit to peeing in the cockpit - on the basis that you don't need to flush: You've got cockpit drains and there'll be a breaking wave along in a minute.

In the end, I gave the job to Eric (the steering bit) and took myself below.

But that still left the question of breakfast time with no breakfast. The obvious solution was to do what they do on proper cruise ships: a second sitting. The first sitting had been at 4.30 a.m. It would be perfectly respectable to have the second sitting four hours later.

However, since this would not give the galley staff sufficient time to soak another serving of "Bircher Muesli", there would have to be a change of menu. For the second sitting, passengers would be served porridge. The idea was well-received: Thick, glutinous hot porridge - with sultanas, and lashings of honey…

I sat in the cockpit, cold and wet, working the tiller as the wind showed no sign of dropping as scheduled and began to fantasise about hot porridge. It's surprisingly easy to make - even without a farmhouse kitchen and a four-oven Aga.

Four dessert spoons of porridge in a saucepan. Add water, coffee whitener and sultanas. Heat and stir. Don't stop stirring. Add more water at will.

Serve with extra honey or demerara sugar to taste and "milk".

When I say "milk", I mean two teaspoonfuls of coffee whitener dissolved in a little hot water and allowed to cool. You really wouldn't know the difference.

Day 44

Thursday 29th May 2025.
54°24.326'N 7°44.871'W.
Wind: W7. Barometer 1018.
Day's run 129M.
Total: 5,051M.
Average: 114.8.
Distance to Destination: 158M.
ETA: 1.4 days = 31st May.

Nearly there! I started making plans - not the important stuff, not getting the Aries off to Amsterdam or whether to risk pouring acid into the engine at anchor outside Douglas. No, the really important stuff - like Indian or Chinese for the first dinner ashore?

By this time, I was in the traffic separation scheme off Ratlin Island. There was no one else in it. Would it really matter if I got my head down for 20 minutes?

Well, nobody was going to know. I had three or four 20-minute kips, fastidiously getting up every time the alarm went off, checking the plotter, having a look around…

Then, at 2.30 in the morning - pitch dark in the cabin (apart from all the glowing and flashing LEDs which light up my night time in the same way that the Aurora Borealis comforts the Inuit), there was the most tremendous *bang* from somewhere.

You shouldn't ignore a loud bang. Tapio Lentinen racing round the world in his Gala 36 Asteria, heard a loud bang down in the Southern Ocean. Two minutes later, he was up to his waist in water. In no time at all, he was in the liferaft - and sat there for 24 hours before being rescued by the eventual race winner, Kirsten Neuschäfer.

My bang wasn't as loud as that. A bolt had broken somewhere, I decided. A headsail sheet car was the obvious culprit (you can blame headsail sheets for most things).

Not a bit of it. When I got out, all dolled up with a head torch on top of everything else, I looked up the deck and there, leaning over the pulpit as if it was being sick, was the headsail.

I could only see a bit of it from the cockpit, but it was quite clear that the forestay had parted.

When that happens, there's one thing to do - and it needs doing pretty darned quickly: Find something else to hold up the mast. Losing the forestay may be regarded as a misfortune. Losing the mast looks like carelessness.

Among *Samsara's* many previous owners was someone who obviously lay awake wondering about this sort of thing, which is why she has a removable inner forestay. Ostensibly, this is to carry the staysail if you want to indulge in the fetish of sporting a cutter rig or fly down the Tradewinds with twin headsails. Otherwise, it is for moments such as this.

All I had to do was release it from its stowage with the starboard shrouds, clip it to its eye-bolt in the centre of the foredeck and wind it up tight.

OK, so it was blowing a light ten knots from aft of the beam, and the sea was pretty much flat. Things could have been a lot worse. For instance, it could have happened in the middle of that big blow in mid-Atlantic. It could have happened in that other big blow off the coast of Northern Ireland. I started thinking about that. Obviously, in that situation, the mast *would* have come down. Imagine having your mast in the water to leeward (it would have fallen to leeward). The boat drifting down onto it. There would be grinding noises from underneath. I would be pulling everything out of the wardrobe locker to get at the bolt cutters.

I've carried these around for years, fretting that they're awkward to stow (one and a half metres long and about 7kg). They rust horribly - and the only time I've ever used them was to cut my bike free when I messed up the combination on Barra - which was pretty stupid really: Nobody steals anything in the Western Isles (where would they take it?)

No, dismasting didn't bear thinking about.

All the same, if you must pick a place to lose your forestay, the middle of a traffic separation scheme isn't exactly ideal either - particularly when there is an enormous cruise ship just coming up behind. It was lit up like a Christmas Tree, as they all are. This one was the *Silver Wind*. I called her up. I had my official seaman-like persona on me. I was going to say I was *Not Under Command* - a wonderful phrase. It gives the impression that I'm some sort of Captain Kirk, suddenly free from the control of The Federation, free to go where no man has gone before…

Silver Wind didn't answer. He just went round me. It was a tremendous disappointment.

Meanwhile, I was going to be busy. The sail was acting like a sea-anchor, pinning us in the same spot. The first thing to do would be to get it out of the water. There was a shackle still holding the furling drum to the stemhead…

That was the easy part. Next, I had to take the sail off. I have never found this particularly easy, even with the mast up: You would expect it just to fall down (gravity being a wonderful thing). But I always had to tug and swear.

It was pointless trying to pull it off horizontally when it was full of water and had the whole weight of the boat pulling in the other direction. In the end, I gathered it in bit by bit, holding it with my chest against the guardrails like a foretopman on the Cutty Sark. After some minutes of this, I was able to get a line round it (would that be a buntline? When did I last have occasion to use the word "buntline"?)

It seemed to take an awfully long time. After a bit, the sun came up - a tentative watery sun. I remember thinking how very fortunate I was that all this had happened now. In fact, thinking about it and doing a proper count, there had been not one, but two gales in the middle of the Atlantic. Heavens, the mast could have gone over the side in some narrow pass among the San Blas islands with coral all around ready to punch holes in the fibreglass...

Once I had everything lashed to the guardrails, I pulled the staysail out of the forepeak (from under the trysail and the storm jib) and bent it onto the inner forestay. The tide had turned - running fast at three or four knots. We were standing still - and that was going to carry on for another three hours of foul tide. Then there would be some strong headwinds due on Saturday morning.

I stood at the chart table working it out - flipping between the Windy app and Navionics. Given the size of the staysail, strong headwinds would be preferable to a calm with an engine that overheated in five minutes. All the same, it is better to see out "strong headwinds" from a restaurant table in Douglas (Chinese or Indian) than in the middle of the Irish Sea.

I decided that we should get there just in time. The forecast was for a beam wind. The problems would start on arrival. I would need some help. With no forestay, no engine - and a whole lot of furling gear hanging out the back, like the bumpkin on the classic lugger that charters out of Falmouth. I wouldn't have anything like the manoeuvrability I was used to.

I just fell asleep - really - I woke up a millisecond before my head hit the keyboard. It's not surprising when you think about it: The sail came down at 2.30 in the morning, and before that, I had been sleeping for thirty minutes at a time…

But the wind came back - and, with it, the sun. By nine o'clock in the morning, we were doing seven knots in the right direction. Breakfast in the cockpit - a lovely day for a sail! In fact, I decided to spend much of it asleep because we'd be arriving in the middle of the night. I'd have to anchor off Douglas and go in tomorrow morning…

I used a bit of Starlink data to check that there's a rigger in the Isle of Man. Google gave me Manx Marine Services, who seem to do everything. It looks as though I can get a new forestay and still arrive in Falmouth in time for the party.

I'm looking forward to finding out what went wrong. This is a new foil. I've only had it for two years. I suspect it's the fastening at the top of the mast that's failed. It hasn't been touched in 50 years. We shall see…

Reasoning that I didn't have far to go, I lashed the sail and furler all together and tied them to the guardrail and then pointed south once more.

We'd missed the tide - and we were slower anyway, the staysail was never much of a sail, particularly in the light winds and calms which is what reality provided in place of the Windy's "Green Wind".

I took a picture of the side deck, the foil with the sail bundled on it reminded me of Hemingway's giant blue marlin in The Old Man and the Sea - too big to get in the boat. I captioned it "Attrition".

Meanwhile, I had a problem: Although the tide was with me, the wind was on the nose. I wasn't actually making much progress - and then, when the tide turned, you could be sure the wind would drop, so I still wouldn't be making much progress.

The forecast didn't help - but, in another 24 hours, I should have a fair wind going from Belfast Lough to the Isle of Man.

So, the plan is to hole up in Ballyholme Bay just by Carrickfergus and leave as early as possible the next day - three o'clock in the morning before it's even properly light - and hope to get in before they close the marina gate at Douglas.

Also, if I'm really keen, I could put the barnacle stuff in the engine, so at least I'd have that working…

Then there was Eric. If I was going to spend a day at anchor, I could ring up the Raymarine helpline - although, that's not so easy when the iPhone tells you it's got water in the charging port and you have to do everything with it sitting on a wireless charger.

Day 45

Friday 30th May 2025.
55°03.264'N 5°36.938'W.
Wind: E1. Barometer: 1010.
Day's Run: 81M.
Total 5,132M.
Average: 114M.
Distance to Destination: 77M.
ETA: 0.6 days = 16.5 hrs = 31st May, 0500.

As an experiment - and also because we happened to be going backwards with the tide at the time - I ran the engine, knowing there wouldn't be any cooling water coming out of the exhaust. I wanted to see how long I could run it before I had to turn it off to stop it overheating and catching fire.

I have an exhaust temperature monitor for this - apparently, overheated exhausts are a major cause of engine fires. The monitor measures the temperature of the rubber hose and sounds an alarm. I had set mine to go off at 50°C (at the engine manufacturer's recommendation of 40°, it just kept on going off all the time.)

I timed it, and at a respectable 1900 revs, it took ten minutes to get up to 48°C.

Well, that would be alright. I could probably get all the way from the outer harbour, over the flap gate and up the channel into the marina in ten minutes.

Then, would you believe, the temperature started dropping! I would be able to get all the way into a berth! It was still at 43°C after 15 minutes. I switched it off then. I didn't want to push my luck.

So, all being well, I should catch the TT, get the forestay fixed and be in Falmouth on schedule.

We'll see.

Day 46

> Saturday 31st May 2025.
> 54°458.370'N 05°19.337'W.
> Wind: SE3. Barometer: 1012.
> Day's Run: 18M. Total 5,069M.
> Average: 110.2M.
> Distance to Destination: 62M.
> ETA: 0.6 days = 1st June 0100hrs.

Slowly, inexorably, we began to make our way into Ballyholme Bay. I sat at the tiller, pretending I was in a Laser, trying to pick up every tiny wind shift. I must say, the staysail is a lovely sail for windward work. It's very flat, so you can sail really close to the wind. In fact, for strong winds, it's a even better sail than the headsail. I think I may get it valeted instead of ordering a new one.

Ballyholme turned out to be a pretty little bay with houses clustered around the shore and one other boat, big Halberg Rassey, waiting just like me.

I was almost within hailing distance when suddenly, for no apparent reason, the depth recorder set itself to feet instead of metres. I am a European. I understand metres. I can't remember how big a foot is (alright, so it's the length of a foot. What else would it be?)

With help from the internet, I managed to find the "settings" and switched it to metres - but then, when I tried to switch it back out of the settings menu, it wouldn't go. Drifting round in circles, I tried pressing every conceivable combination of buttons, but couldn't get back to the main menu. I was left with the word "metres" but no numbers. I thought: How am I going to anchor?

...and then answered myself: "I'll just look at the chart and add a bit for good measure."

I was all ready to do that, when I thought: "I know what I'll do, I'll ring Raymarine." But of course, it was a Saturday. So, that was no good.

But there was always Dave Jones in North Wales. "Call any time," he had said.

I left a message.

In the end, I was struck by the brilliant and simple idea of turning the thing off at the mains and - Bingo! Back to metres. I sent Dave an email saying it was all fixed and not to worry, but later he rang anyway, and we had a good chat (my first conversation in 47 days, I worked out afterwards. No wonder I was so chatty). He had been tracking me on one of the shipfinder apps - which are not as good as PolarSteps which provides a track as well as a current position.

The other thing about the ship-tracking app was that it gave my starting point as Colombia, and Dave thought that maybe the UK Border Force might be quite interested in that, given Colombia's best-known export.

While all this was going on, the cabin was an absolute tip - the aftermath of the engine investigations. You can imagine what it looked like by the time I came to let go the anchor - and discovered that all those gales had thrown the boat's head around so much that the chain was now as tangled as my grandmother's knitting basket after the kitten go at it.

Of course, I should have thought of this and given myself time to sort it out as we sailed sedately towards the bay. In the event, I was completely taken by surprise and stood on the foredeck, yanking and swearing, just like all the other times - I daresay much to the amusement of the Halberg Rassey crew.

In the end, I had to get into the chain locker and untangle it one link at a time - and while I was doing that, I discovered the locker was half-full of water and all the chain was rusty. I thought: "My God, what a terrible waste!"

This was new chain only a year or so ago. I had to investigate that before things got any worse - why was the limber hole not working?

What I discovered was that at the bottom of the locker is a triangular piece of wood with a hole in it. If you take this out, you may well find two cereal bowlsful of mud. Well, I found enough mud to fill two cereal bowls. I hadn't actually brought a cereal bowl with me. I just ladled it into my other hand until it couldn't hold any more, and then staggered out and threw it over the side - checked that we didn't seem to be drifting into trouble - and then fetched a cereal bowl for the rest.

Once I got all the mud out, the water drained away obediently, so obviously it does go somewhere. By the time I had re-assembled the chain locker, I was a bit behind schedule, but it was still only two o'clock in the afternoon, so I thought I had time to do the muriatic acid thing. Of course, first I had to get the pump set up with all its electrical connections.

I was busy making electrical connections under the chart table - never my favourite place - and the little terminals were just too big to fit in the little slots, so I had to cut the terminals and it took forever - and then I needed hose (which I could have got from the cockpit locker or even under the sink, but the only hose I could think about was under the starboard focsle berth, so everything had to come out of there) - and by the time Dave rang back, it was four o'clock and the cabin was even more of a tip - and I still hadn't got the engine running.

I tried playing with the seacock to see if that made any difference, but it just unwound. I was a bit anxious that if I kept on unwinding it, the tap would come off and the water would come in, so I stopped doing that.

By this time, I was thinking it was all getting rather late and I had to be up very, very early in the morning, and I wanted to have a nice dinner at the table - and, oh my! We were still drifting around…

The great feature of dinner in Ballyholme Bay was the final two-thirds of the last onion - so basically all the onions - and a stone-cold bottle of wine from the locker under my berth. It was clearly past its best (although I had three glasses to taste before I started cooking).

The other thing about dinner was that it had to be rice because I didn't have anything else - no pasta, no mashed potatoes. It turned out that the answer to eating your way through an insect infestation (and please remember this, you may need it one day) is rinsing the rice with several changes of water. The bugs float to the top. You can skim them off with a spoon.

I kept skimming and changing the water and skimming and changing. There was a lot of dust in there as well (probably bug shit), but in the end, it looked all right, so I ate it.

The original plan had been to leave at four in the morning. I set the alarm for quarter past three and, looking at the weather. I didn't want to arrive too soon, so I decided to leave a bit later and have breakfast first - with the luxury of sitting at the table.

So, breakfast was at half past four or something, and I finally left at five, which meant that by lunchtime - or what would have been lunchtime - I was going to be seriously hungry. But I thought: "No, no; I'm looking forward to my dinner ashore tonight…

Of course, I succumbed and, as if to make it less of a meal, had the most disgusting thing I could find, which turned out to be a tin of Panamanian mixed vegetables (some rather strangely-coloured peas and diced carrots). I didn't heat it up, just put it in a cereal bowl and poured Salsa Inglesa over the top. Salsa Inglesa is the mock Lee and Perrins. It didn't do anything for cold mixed vegetables, so I tried Salsa Negra, which doesn't really taste of anything at all. The final third went down with chilli sauce.

Day 47

> Sunday 1st June 2025.
> 54°31.379'N 43° 43.458'W.
> Wind: SW5. Barometer 1009.
> Day's Run: 32M.
> Total 5,101M.
> Average: 108.5M.
> Distance to Destination: 32M.
> ETA: 0.3days = 1st June 2000hrs.

By the time I finished the disgusting lunch, we were arriving at the Isle of Man and that very strange lighthouse on the north eastern end, which is set back from the shore, so that as you go round it appears to stay with you as if you're not making any progress at all.

Obligingly, the wind veered and we had a good run down to Douglas, although there were some tremendous gusts as the wind funnelled through the mountains. I kept *Samsara* reefed virtually all the way.

I should have kept her reefed right to the end, but shook it out at the north end of Douglas Bay since there weren't any more mountains. I should have known that when I got to the harbour entrance, it would be blowing like stink.

I still didn't have an engine I could rely on, so I needed to sail as close as possible to the harbour mouth - possibly even into the harbour… in which case I decided (rather belatedly) that I did need that reef after all.

This operation was complicated by a small cruise ship anchored just off the harbour mouth. First, I tried to reef upwind of her, then decided I was getting too close, so gybed round her stern with the halyard still slack and the sail half collapsed like a clown's trousers - at which point a man in a harbourmaster's RIB approached and started shouting. I couldn't hear a word he said against the wind and the flapping mainsail, but eventually all the gesticulating prompted me to look out to seaward - where the Isle of Man ferry was approaching at speed.

Never mind; I gesticulated inshore, indicating that I would go there while the ferry docked - and while I was doing it, I managed to make contact with Harbour Control and, in a long transmission, informed them that I had no engine and proposed to sail into the harbour.

They were very understanding about all this - particularly since, once I had eased in between the moles and dropped the sails all over the deck and finally made my hesitant way (stop-starting the engine) to the waiting pontoon, Rory from the harbour office turned up. In the friendliest and most helpful fashion - this is the Isle of Man after all - he explained that my arrival without any VHF communication just as the ferry was due had caused all kinds of consternation - and, next time, please would I announce myself an hour before arrival… if there is a next time…

Meanwhile, I had been looking forward to dinner ashore, but I had to clear customs first. I did consider just not mentioning it, but that could get me into all kinds of trouble. Following the correct protocol means flying the yellow Q flag (my vessel is healthy and I require free pratique) and reporting to customs. I imagine I can't do that until Monday morning, so I suppose I shall have to stay on the pontoon outside the marina and go in then - in which case, I shall see if I can get a takeaway delivered.

I'm rather looking forward to that. I might even watch Breakfast at Tiffany's, which has just popped up on Netflix - that sounds about right over an Indian. As it turned out, the equally charming Vicky and Silver came with their customs forms. They had been up at the airport and thought: "Why not clear the little yacht before going home?"

But I still couldn't go ashore because the German boat inside me wanted to leave - but only when they'd finished dinner… and then when they'd washed up… and then once they'd taken my picture.

In the end, I didn't get ashore until nine o'clock, heading for the only Indian restaurant I could find on the internet that would stay open until ten. It's just that I didn't realise how far it was to the Aura Bar and Restaurant (Indian fusion, beer and cocktails).

Maybe it wasn't really that far, but on the other hand, I hadn't walked any further than 9.7metres for the last 47 days. By the time I managed a hundred yards, my legs wanted to seize up.

The next morning - Monday, I was all ready to find someone to fix the engine so I could motor into the marina, when I realised that I'm approaching this all wrong. You don't get French celebrity singlehanders worrying about where to find people to fix things. French celebrity singlehanders step off their boats straight into the TV studio while their team of "preparateurs" take care of everything they broke along the way.

And it turns out I have a "preparateur" too. His name is Tony Jones. He's the rigger who works out of an ancient van in Conwy. He replaced all my rigging in the big refit two years ago.

Now he was in Douglas, leaning his bike up against the railing and saying: "What have you done with your forestay?"

Tony notices these things.

Two minutes later, we were down on the pontoon, taking the sail off the furling gear so that he could dismantle it (with a good deal of grumbling about the state of my Allen keys).

All I have to do now is sail over to Conwy (55 miles with a south westerly on the beam) and he will have new bearings ordered, a new forestay made up and put the whole thing back together - making sure the super zero halyard doesn't break it again by pressing on it on port tack, which he reckons is probably what happened.

We were still mulling over this and talking about motorbikes - Tony's passion too - when Craig the harbourmaster turned up and announced: "You can't stay here. It's coming on to blow tonight, and the swell comes round the eastern mole - and heaven help you if the lifeboat gets a shout and steams past at twelve knots.

So, he brought his little launch and tied it alongside and squeezed me into the marina.

And so began the long, long process of getting everything else fixed. Most important, of course, was the engine, because without the engine, I would have to be towed out again, and I couldn't expect Craig to go through all that again.

The problem is that nothing much happens on the Isler of Man during TT week - at least nothing that doesn't involve very large and noisy motorcycles. Eventually, I found a wild Scotsman called Rab McCluskey who said he would come - but then he couldn't and then he didn't and then they closed the roads just as he was going to - and after that he had to go and collect his wife and they live right on the course and so as soon as the racing starts, they're marooned.

He was going to come on the Tuesday while it was raining, but he got pulled over by the police because he'd forgotten to tax his car.

Finally, he came on Wednesday, and we established there was some sort of blockage in the cooling water - but no sooner had we reached that conclusion than it stopped raining, and the racing was on again, and that meant Rab had to go and pick up his wife before they closed the roads.

By Thursday, when he still hadn't reappeared, I was beginning to get just a little frustrated and thinking this wasn't going to work at all, particularly since a very nice electrician called Ben turned up and told me why the pressurised water wasn't working and I couldn't flush the watermaker (it's just the daft little pressure switch on the bottom which is supposed to register the drop in pressure when you turn on a tap. Of course, it doesn't, but don't worry, we can bypass it. If you want to turn on the pump, you just flick the switch.)

He said he couldn't really charge me for that, bless him.

But still no Rab. I got out the muriatic acid. I had been researching it online - the correct proportions and all that sort of thing. Some people seemed to think it's OK. Some said I mustn't use it without an inhibitor (what's an inhibitor, it sounds like something to restrain an embarrassing uncle at a wedding.)

In the end, I made up a 10:1 solution and poured that down the pipe. It just sat there - which meant I had to get it out again. It was all a bit of a disaster, really.

I found a company with a fleet of (taxed) vans and an engineer who wasn't married to come and have a look.

Only he didn't.

Craig said there was a follower of the blog who was always going on about the miracle health supplement, who wanted to meet me.

"He's very handy," said Craig.

I don't know if he ever did come because I spent the next two days leaning on a fence watching motorbikes whip past me at 160miles an hour. (A marshal suggested I keep my hands inside the fence).

In the end, I fixed the engine with a citric acid recipe I found on the internet. Whatever was in there came out green.

It meant I could set off to Conwy and meet Tony for the new forestay. Besides, it was Saturday, the final day of racing with three new records to show for the event.

Michael Dunlop set three, including 123.056mph in the Supertwin class. The Crowe brothers became the first sidecar pair to break 121mph on the mountain course - and Dean Harrison recorded the fastest ever lap in the night qualifying session at 133.069mph.

And John Passmore sailed 5,133 miles in 47 days at an average speed of 108.5 miles a day, including a new record day's run of 150 miles over the ground.

The End

Amazon Stars & Reviews

These are so important. Nobody buys a book on Amazon if it doesn't have enough stars.

If you are reading this on Kindle, you will be invited to leave between one star and five stars. Fill them in, and your device will upload them next time you're connected.

If you have the paperback edition, the person who bought it can award stars by finding the book on their Amazon "My Orders" page.

Good books tend to have at least 4½ stars – and since there are always going to be some people who object violently to something or other and leave only one star, the only way to get to 4½ is for the people who really do like it to leave 5 stars.

So, if you feel this one deserves 5 stars, then that would be an enormous help.

Next there are the reviews. Most readers will look through half a dozen. Finding that a diverse group of people have been moved to write thoughtfully and in detail about what they have read is reassuring for someone unfamiliar with the author's work.

It doesn't do the author's ego any harm, either.

Thank you.

JP

Books by the Same Author

Old Man Sailing: Some Dreams Take A Lifetime

When COVID-19 struck the UK, the government advised the over-70s to "shield" while the country went into Lockdown. One old man went sailing instead. Single-handed and self-isolated, retired journalist John Passmore used the pandemic to achieve an ambition which had eluded him for 60 years. For 3,629 miles, he disappeared into a world of perfect solitude, adventure and adversity – arriving back 42 days later, short of water and with shredded sails to find himself celebrated on national radio as the embodiment of everybody's Lockdown dream. This is his story. It is also a story for anyone who ever thought a dream was unattainable.

A word-of-mouth bestseller - *Yachting Monthly*

This title is also available in French as: *Le vieil homme hisse la voile.*

The Voyage #1: BVIs to Falmouth

This is what it is like to sail an ocean alone. Not the world-girdling marathon of the Southern Ocean racers or the "cruise in company" as part of a trade-wind rally, but what it is really like to set off for 3,496 miles from the British Virgin Islands to Falmouth in the UK, totally alone.

That means no contact with the shore, no high-frequency radio or satphone. No weather forecasts, no texts from loved ones. No news….

Just complete and uninterrupted isolation for 44 days.

In other words, this is singlehanded ocean sailing at its purest: One man in a world shrunk to its bare essentials.

John Passmore is a life-long sailor and professional writer. His book Old Man Sailing was described by *Yachting Monthly* as "a word-of-mouth bestseller."

In *The Voyage,* he takes it a step further. At times truly hilarious, at others, quite frankly weird; as Yachting World's Tom Cunliffe said of the author: "A professional storyteller who always sees the funny side, even when laughs must have been hard to find."

Audiobook available from the oldmansailing website.

The Voyage #2: Falmouth to Grenada

The Voyage #1 was a success – even though nothing happened. It turned out that readers liked the easy style – the sideways view of a singlehanded ocean crossing in a small boat without long-range communications. No news, no weather forecasts. Just one man and his boat in the middle of nowhere.

As one Amazon reviewer put it: "The man can write. Entertaining and fun. Makes you wish you had the courage to do this too. He turns every disaster into an opportunity. Great character and great attitude."

So here is The Voyage #2 – and this time something did happen: A knockdown, a broken rudder, 1,500 miles with the steering held together with string…

The Good Stuff – Book One

John Passmore is the author of *Old Man Sailing: Some Dreams Take a Lifetime* – the story of his escape from Lockdown by sailing alone into the Atlantic for 42 days and 3,629 miles. Yachting Monthly called it "A word-of-mouth bestseller". Many of the five-star reviews claimed it worked so well because there was more to the story than the adventure: There were humorous anecdotes. There was a love story…

What the readers did not know was that all of this was chronicled in detail as it happened. Throughout the early 80s and into the noughties, Passmore was writing for yachting magazines and national newspapers.

Here, for the first time, is a complete and chronological account: Everything from levitating the dog and navigating by smell to meeting his wife, Tamsin, through the Lonely Hearts column of Time Out and attempting to run away to sea and raise a family on a 27ft boat.

It is a laugh-out-loud, real-life story of love and exasperation afloat – when it's not making you cry. It is, as the editor of Yachting World said at the time – "Good Stuff."

The Good Stuff – Book Two

In this second volume of The Good Stuff, John and Tamsin have a baby on the boat – and then another one. The idyllic lifestyle, sailing where the wind blows them, sitting over a glass of wine as the sun turns the estuary to liquid gold is suddenly more complicated. Where do you find a launderette in the middle of the French countryside? How do you keep to the maintenance schedule with help from a two-year-old?

At least it was good copy. There was Yachting World's *Dogwatch* column to feed every month and the Daily Telegraph's travel page. Apparently, the readers were captivated by the couple's determination to put a brave face on even the most desperate situation – or maybe they just liked the dog.

Here you will discover how to win third prize in the Tayvallich Regatta one-oar race and what the home counties school nurse said to the Liverpool "Scally". And where else do you think you would find detailed instructions for casting *The Curse of the Stones* on troublesome neighbours?

It is, as the editor of *Yachting World* said at the time – Good Stuff.

Trident: The Future Is Out of Control – And It's Happening Now

A new Prime Minister committed to scrapping Britain's nuclear deterrent - a Russian president meddling in other countries' elections and an isolationist in the White House...Does any of this sound familiar?

John Passmore's prescient novel, written in the 1980's and set in what was then the future, suddenly becomes terrifyingly relevant today.As NATO collapses and Russia looks to the West, the future of the world rests in the hands of a submarine captain, his aged father, an old-fashioned reporter and a government secretary in love with a man who is not what he seems..."Fast-moving and immensely prescient, there are echoes of the early works of Ken Follett and Frederick Forsyth." - *Daily Mail*

Faster, Louder, Riskier, Sexier

As a top-flight foreign correspondent, John Passmore was at the pinnacle of his career: The Chief Correspondent of the London Evening Standard. Then, at the age of 45, he announced that he was bored and resigned.

It would not be until he was 68 that this made any sense. It turned out that he had ADHD. In fact, his particular condition was in the 1% of the most severe cases.

Suddenly, everything made sense – the chronic search for excitement, the chaotic relationships, bad driving, his complete inability to remember anyone's name…

It is a startling thing to have your whole life explained to you when you are practically in your dotage. Indeed, it can be a crushing emotional experience.

Passmore dealt with it the only way he knew how. He wrote about it. He wrote about it with all the urgency and passion he brought to his newspaper despatches. He filled it with the humour that had been his trademark.

From farmworker and door-to-door salesman to singlehanded sailor and network marketer, he came to terms with a mental kink which affects 5% of the world's population. Indeed, he learned to embrace it.

If you are one of the 1.5 billion people in the world with ADHD – or if you live with one of them – you need this book.

If you just want to laugh out loud at the story of the *Load of Straw*, you need this book.

ADHD MLM: Why Network Marketing Is Perfect for Weirdos - And How to Make It Work When Nothing Else Does

There are 1.5 billion people in the world with ADHD – and a whole lot more who just don't have enough money. But it's the other 6.5 billion who make the rules. Hardly surprising the weirdos have a hard time fitting in.

Getting a job can be difficult if you keep blurting out responses in interviews and fill in application forms with a lot of crossings out.

Keeping a job is no easier if you can't follow instructions, are bored by repetitive tasks and don't seem to get along with your coworkers (whose names you keep forgetting anyway).

And all of that would be OK if only you could manage on a small income instead of constantly splurging on pointless purchases.

If any of this seems familiar, you need this book. With Network Marketing, MLM or whatever your Home-Based business wants to call itself, you don't have to pass an interview. You don't have a boss. Whether you succeed or fail is entirely down to you.

But how are you supposed to succeed when Network Marketing (like everything else) was designed for people whose minds don't keep wandering off in random directions just when they're supposed to be paying attention?

I'm John Passmore and I have had ADHD all my life. I didn't know until I was 68 years old (and they told me mine was in the 1% of the most severe cases). But by that time, I had reached the top 0.2% of my Network Marketing company. I did it by ignoring all the rules and developing a completely new way of doing things.

It's a system that will work for you too – whatever type of home business you're in.

And that's guaranteed: Either this works or you get your money back. Which is just as well, because this is a very expensive book. There's a reason: I could have put the same information into an online course and charged $999 for it. But I think the people who publish online courses probably make more from them than they do from Network Marketing. I am a Network Marketer, not an internet entrepreneur. Also, I want people to value the information - that's why there's the money-back guarantee.

Anyway, you can always download a sample and find out what it's all about before you spend any money at all...

Printed in Dunstable, United Kingdom